NOTE TO PARENTS

Some of these projects require tools or materials that can be dangerous if used improperly. Adult supervision will be necessary when projects require the use of scissors, a craft knife, varnish, turpentine, a hot iron, an oven, or pins and needles. Before children start a project, you may want to cover the work space with sheets of newspaper or a plastic cloth to make cleaning up easier. You may also want them to wear an apron or an old shirt to protect their clothing. We recommend using a piece of thick cardboard as a cutting board when working with craft knifes.

Please discuss safety with your children, and note in advance which projects will require your supervision.

ACKNOWLEDGMENTS

All photographs by David Johnson

FUN WITH FABRIC

Projects made by Jan Bridge and Anne Sharples
Illustrations by Joanna Venus

FUN WITH PAINT

Paintings made by Brian Robertson, Katie Scampton,
and Anne Sharples
Illustrations by Elizabeth Kerr and Joanna Venus

FUN WITH PAPER

Paper models made by Karen Radford,
Brian Robertson, and Anne Sharples
Illustrations by Joanna Venus

MAKING PRESENTS

Presents made by Karen Radford,
Anne Marie Mulligan, and Anne Sharples
Illustrations by Elizabeth Kerr

HAMLYN CHILDREN'S BOOKS

Series Editor: Anne Civardi
Series Designer: Anne Sharples
Production Controller: Linda Spillane

CREATIVE CRAFTS

FUN WITH FABRIC
and
MAKING PRESENTS
by Juliet Bawden

FUN WITH PAINT by Moira Butterfield

FUN WITH PAPER by Heather Amery

CONTENTS

FUN WITH PAPER

FUN WITH PAINT

FUN WITH FABRIC

MAKING PRESENTS

• CREATIVE CRAFTS •

FUN WITH
PAPER

• HEATHER AMERY •

MATERIALS, TIPS, AND HINTS

In this section there are lots of fantastic things for you to make with paper and cardboard. It is a good idea to keep a big cardboard box of useful things, such as toilet paper rolls, paper towel rolls, tinfoil rolls, wrapping paper, empty chocolate boxes, cereal boxes, cardboard boxes, and scraps of wallpaper and tissue paper. Then you will have the things you need when you want to make something.

Collect magazines, catalogs, and travel brochures with color pictures. Cut out pictures of flowers, trees, scenes or anything you like that might be nice to decorate cards or boxes.

Pieces of gold and silver foil from candy wrappers may be useful.

You can buy sheets of construction paper, tissue paper, crepe paper and posterboard in bright colors.

Collect thin and thick cardboard from old calendars, thick envelopes, and junk mail.

Scissors

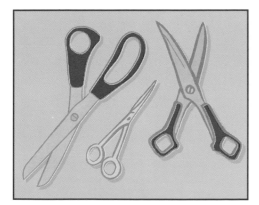

You will need scissors for cutting paper. You will need sharp, pointed ones to make holes in paper and cardboard. For cutting very small or delicate things, use small scissors.

X-Acto knife

Ask an adult to help if you use an X-Acto knife for cutting paper or cardboard. Always use a piece of cardboard as a cutting board, and press downward.

Paints and crayons

Poster, tempera, and watercolor paints, felt-tip pens, and crayons are all useful for decorating things and for writing messages on cards or posters.

String and tape

If you only have white string, you can color it with watered-down paint. Let it dry on a sheet of newspaper. You can use double-stick tape instead of glue.

Glue

Buy a jar of children's paste. It is easy to use and has a brush. You can also buy glue with a thin tube at the top so you can squeeze a little out at a time. It is less messy.

HANDY HINTS

Making things can be messy. Before you start, put sheets of old newspaper on the top of the table or floor. And remember to clean up when you have finished. Pick up all the bits of paper that are sticky with glue.

Remember to put the tops and lids back on glue containers, paints, and felt-tip pens so that these materials don't dry out. Wash any glue off your fingers. Otherwise they will get dirty and leave finger marks everywhere.

Keep a ruler handy for measuring things and for drawing and cutting straight lines.

BRILLIANT BOXES

Boxes and baskets are great for keeping all sorts of things in and for packing up presents. These are made out of posterboard and covered with colored paper or decorated with paint. You can make them any size, from very shallow to quite deep, with lids for the boxes.

Decorate the boxes with stars, paper bows, or a pretty border.

Things you need

Posterboard or cardboard
Colored paper
Pencil and ruler
Watercolor or poster paints
Scissors
Tape and strong glue

Shallow box

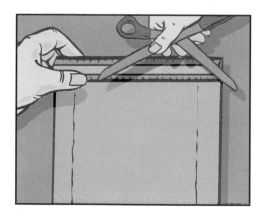

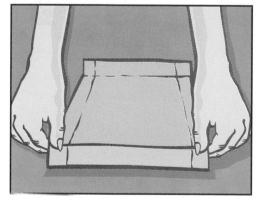

1. Hold a ruler down on one side of the posterboard, 12 in. x 8 in. Run scissors along the ruler's other edge to make a groove. Do this to all four sides.

2. Carefully fold up one side of the posterboard along the line of the groove, like this. Unfold it and then carefully fold up the other three sides, one at a time.

3. Unfold the piece of posterboard and cut along the groove at each corner, as shown. Stop when you reach the groove going the other way.

Paint patterns or flowers, or stick paper shapes on your baskets.

Fold colored paper around a box. Make a cut at each corner. Tuck in the tabs and glue the paper to the box.

Bright basket

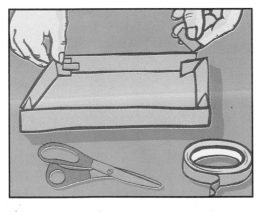

4. Fold up the posterboard into a box shape, with the tabs on the inside, as shown. Tape the tabs to the side of the box, or you can staple or glue them.

5. To make the box lid, make another box. But put the ruler just over the edge of the posterboard when you groove it so that the lid is a little bigger.

To make a deep, square basket, fold the posterboard into a box shape, keeping the sides slanted. Glue the sides together and trim the corners. Glue on a handle.

11

PAPER JEWELS

These paper beads are very easy to make and look like exotic jewelry. Thread them onto colored string to make necklaces or onto thin elastic to make bracelets. Long, thin beads, or two or three small, fat ones, look good as earrings. Try making the beads with the advertisements cut out of magazines or the Sunday comics.

Things you need

Sheets of colorful or
  patterned paper
Sheets of plain colored paper
Pieces of colored string (about
  2 ft. long)
Thin elastic
Earring fixings (from bead
  or craft shops)
Scissors and glue
Beads

Thread plastic or wooden beads onto your necklace.

Thread different-sized paper beads together.

Striped bead necklace

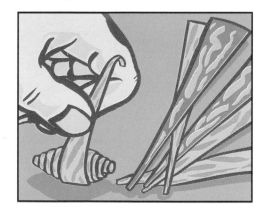

1. Cut out long strips of striped paper that are wide at one end and narrow at the other. Starting at the wide end, roll up a strip with your fingers. Leave a small hole in the middle.

2. When you reach the end of the strip, dab a little glue on the end and press it down gently. Do not squash the bead. Make lots of beads in different-colored stripes and different sizes.

3. Push a big bead onto some string or thin elastic. Put smaller beads on each side. Then thread more beads until you have made a necklace. Leave enough string at each end to tie a bow.

HANDY HINTS

Instead of rolling up the beads with your fingers, try rolling them around a thin knitting needle, a pencil, or a thin stick.

If you want to make a very fat bead, glue two strips of paper together before you roll them up. You can also use thick paper, such as leftover pieces of patterned or plain wallpaper.

To make your jewels, use paper that is colored on both sides or glue two different-colored strips together, back to back.

Easy earrings

1. Cut out a small circle of colored paper. Cut it in half. Roll each half into a long, thin cone. Glue down the ends. Make a hole through the thin end and attach an earring fixing.

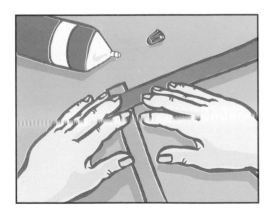

Make a necklace out of different-colored beads.

Make a bracelet with long strips of shiny wrapping paper.

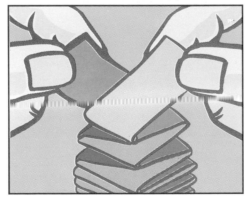

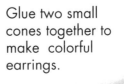

Glue two small cones together to make colorful earrings.

Folded bracelet

1. Cut two strips of colored paper, each about ¾ in. wide and 2 ft. long. Dab glue on the end of one strip and put the other strip at a right angle to it, as shown. Press it down on the glue.

2. Fold the underneath strip over and press it down. Now fold the other strip over and press it down. Fold over the strips until you reach the ends. Glue the ends together.

PERKY PAPER DOLLS

You can make a chain of paper dolls long enough to go around a room for party decorations, or short enough to wrap around boxes and lampshades. If you use plain paper, you can color them with paints or crayons. Colored or patterned paper also makes pretty paper dolls.

Things you need

Long strips of plain or
  patterned paper
Pencil, paints,
  or crayons
Glue and tape
Scissors
Lacy paper

To decorate a lampshade, cut out and glue on two shapes together so they bend around the curve.

Cover a plain box with little paper decorations to make it look special.

Singing girls

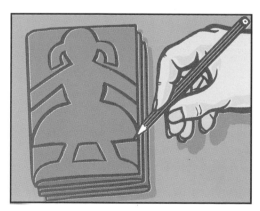

1. Cut out a long strip of plain paper, about 4 in. wide. Fold it up, backward and forward, like an accordian. Make each fold about 4 in. wide.

2. Draw the shape of a little girl wearing a dress on the top piece of paper, like this. Make sure the shape reaches to each side of the paper at the folds.

3. Hold the folded strip of paper firmly and cut out the little girl shape. Leave a small uncut piece where the shape meets at the folds on each side.

A band of singing girls

Tape different-colored strips of paper together to make these flowers.

Black cat chain

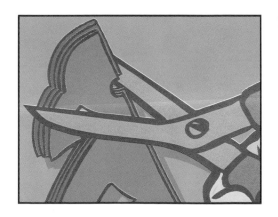

4. To cut out the singing mouths in the girls' faces, fold the paper over sideways down the middle of the face, as shown. Carefully cut out a tiny hole.

5. Make collars out of lacy paper and glue them around the girls' necks. Cut out different-colored paper belts and aprons and glue them onto the dresses, as shown.

6. Cut out two tiny paper eyes for each girl and glue them on their faces. Glue the ends of the strips together to make a long chain to hang up in a room.

FANTASTIC FLOWERS

Paper flowers look bright and cheerful in big bunches tied with a bow, or arranged in a vase or small basket. Try using different-colored crepe paper to make the petals for different kinds of flowers. You can make them in all sorts of shapes and sizes.

Things you need

Crepe paper in different
  colors
Stiff paper for leaves
Thin garden wire
  or florist's wire
Paper towels
Scissors, tape, and glue

Make small paper centers for these daffodils. Tape on yellow or white petals and green leaves.

Color the flower centers with paint or felt-tip pens.

Use a big bright button as a flower center.

HANDY HINTS

When you have finished making a flower and the glue is dry, hold the edges of each petal and gently pull it apart. This stretches the paper and makes the petals rounded.

Cut the wire with old scissors. If it is difficult, ask an adult to help you.

Try using thin sticks instead of wire to make the flower stems.

Perfect petals

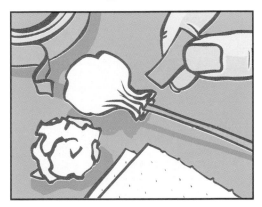

1. Screw up a little piece of paper towel into a ball. Cover it with another piece. Then tape it to one end of a strip of wire, about 10 in. long.

2. Cut a long strip of crepe paper, about 2½ in. wide. Fold it into squares. Cut out petal shapes. You will need at least five petals for each flower.

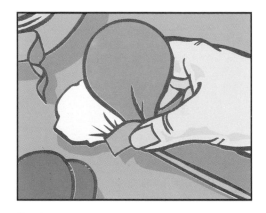

3. Stick a small piece of tape on the bottom of a petal. Tape the petal onto the wire, close to the paper ball. Tape on more petals, overlapping each one.

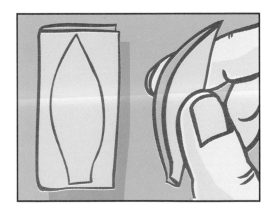

4. Fold a sheet of paper into rectangles. Cut out these leaf shapes. Fold each leaf in half. Crease them down the middle.

5. Cut a long thin strip of crepe paper. Tape one end under the flower. Wind the strip tightly around the wire, to the bottom. Tape down the end.

6. Dab glue on the end of a leaf and stick it under the flower. Glue on two more leaves. Then glue leaves down the stem of the flower, as shown.

17

BRIGHT BLOOMS

Here are more paper flowers that are quick and easy to make. You can use them to decorate all sorts of things, such as tables, presents, and branches or twigs. Make them any size you like, from tiny ones that look like flower buds to much bigger ones like these prize carnations.

Things you need

Crepe paper
Stiff paper for leaves
Tape, glue, and scissors

To make a wreath, draw and cut a big ring out of some stiff paper. Glue flowers and leaves around the ring.

Stick colorful flowers on a present.

18

Colorful carnations

1. Cut a strip, about 3 in. wide, off the top of a folded packet of crepe paper, as shown. Unfold the long strip of paper and flatten it out.

2. Cut a rectangle of stiff paper, 6 in. wide and 10 in. long. Roll it up into a thin tube and glue down the edge. This is the flower stem.

3. Dab glue on one end of the stem. Press the end of the crepe-paper strip onto the glue. Wind the crepe strip around and around the stem.

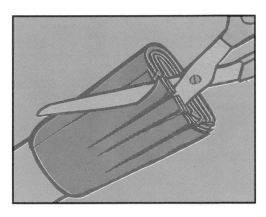

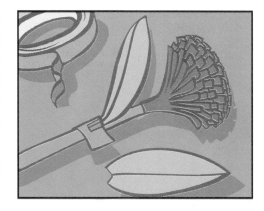

4. Glue down the end of the strip. Put the end of the scissors into the middle of the crepe paper and cut thin strips all the way around, as shown.

5. Pull the strips outward and bend them down a little to look like the petals of a flower. If the flower stem shows at the center, cut it into thin strips.

6. Fold a piece of stiff paper in half. Cut out two leaf shapes. Fold the two leaves in half. Then stick them onto the top of the stem with tape or glue.

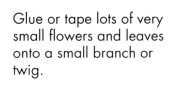

Glue or tape lots of very small flowers and leaves onto a small branch or twig.

HANDY HINTS

To make the flower stems, you can wrap the paper around a thin knitting needle.

Make some carnations with short stems and arrange them in a basket to use as a pretty table decoration.

HIGH FLIERS

Surprise your family and friends by making a bird, a beautiful butterfly, or a black bat fly across a room. You can make it fly very fast or flutter slowly. Use colored paper or white paper that you can paint with bright watercolor or poster paints.

Things you need

Stiff white or
  colored paper
Small curtain ring
Very thin nylon string or
  fishing line
Tape and glue
Scissors
Watercolor or
  poster paints
Pencil

Use different-colored papers to make a bird.

Beautiful butterfly

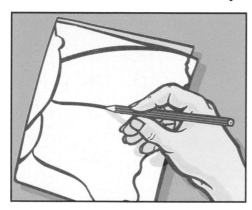

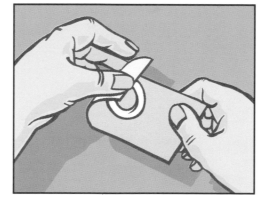

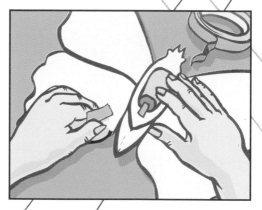

1. Fold a sheet of paper in half. Draw a butterfly's wing on it, and half a butterfly's body on the fold of the paper, as shown. Cut the shape out. Unfold the paper butterfly and flatten it out.

2. Cut out a strip of paper, about 2 in. wide. Roll it around the curtain ring and glue the end down. Make sure the ring is standing upright in the tube of paper, as shown.

3. Push a piece of tape through the paper tube. Press the ends onto the butterfly's body, as shown. Tape on more pieces until the tube is securely attached to the body.

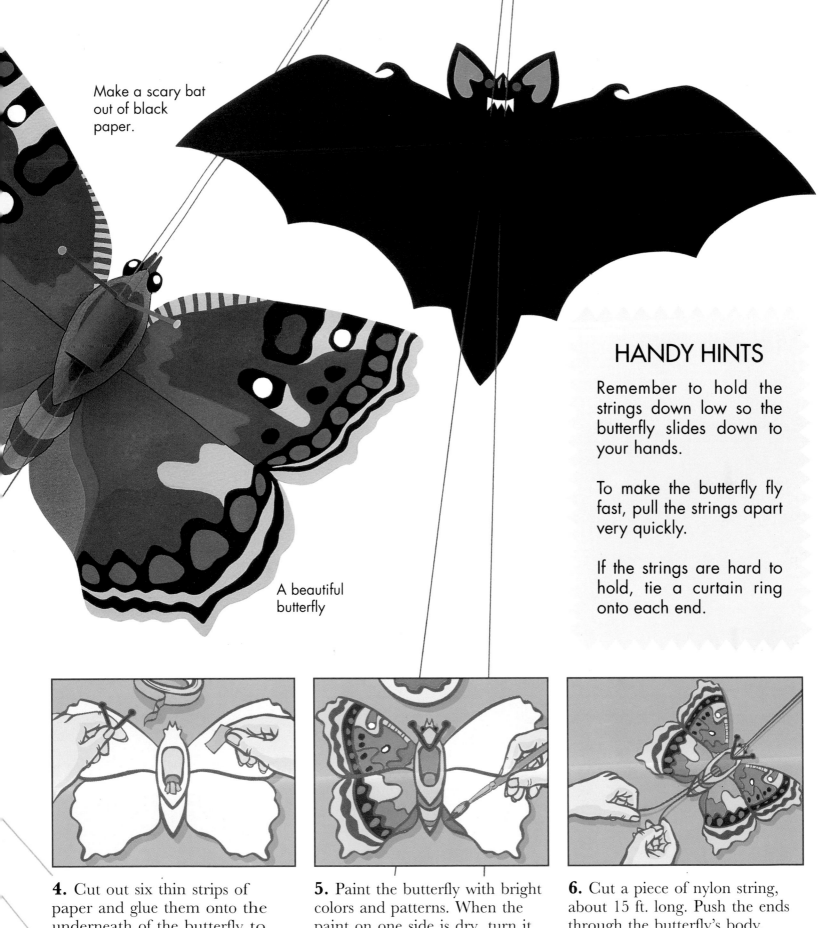

Make a scary bat out of black paper.

A beautiful butterfly

HANDY HINTS

Remember to hold the strings down low so the butterfly slides down to your hands.

To make the butterfly fly fast, pull the strings apart very quickly.

If the strings are hard to hold, tie a curtain ring onto each end.

4. Cut out six thin strips of paper and glue them onto the underneath of the butterfly to make the legs. Glue two thin strips on top of the paper tube to make its antennae.

5. Paint the butterfly with bright colors and patterns. When the paint on one side is dry, turn it over and paint the other side. Hang it up in a safe place and let it dry.

6. Cut a piece of nylon string, about 15 ft. long. Push the ends through the butterfly's body. Loop the string over a hook on the wall or door. Pull the ends of the string apart to make it fly.

FRILLY FOREST

This is a tree you can make any size you like. You could make a big one to put on a table as a centerpiece, or a row of little ones for your room. You could also make lots of different-colored trees. Try decorating them with stars cut out of silver or gold paper.

Things you need

Large sheet of thin cardboard or thick paper about 19 in. long and 9½ in. wide
Cardboard tube from a roll of paper towels or foil
Crepe paper
Two pencils and string
Scissors and glue

Use gold and red paper to make shiny fir trees for Christmas decorations.

Use the tubes from toilet paper rolls to make the trunks of small trees.

Use different colors to make a bright tree.

Fringed fir tree

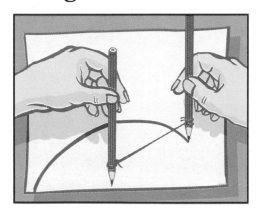

1. Tie the ends of the string to the two pencils. Put one pencil down on the edge of the paper. Draw a half-circle with the other.

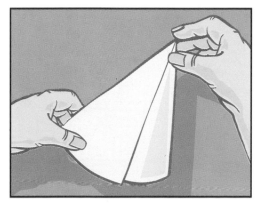

2. Cut out the half-circle of paper and roll it around. Glue the two straight edges together to make a cone, as shown.

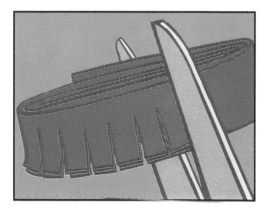

3. Cut long strips of crepe paper, about 2 in. wide. Fold each strip and make cuts along one edge, as shown.

Cover a tree with gold, red, or silver stars and lots of candles.

HANDY HINTS

When drawing circles or half-circles with string and two pencils, shorten or lengthen the string so it is half the length of the cardboard.

Cover the cardboard tube with brown paper or paint it brown to make it look like a tree trunk.

To make small trees, use a plate to draw half circles on the cardboard.

You can use almost any kind of paper to make these fir trees. Wrapping paper, shiny paper, and newspaper all make good trees.

Glue small trees in rows on a piece of cardboard.

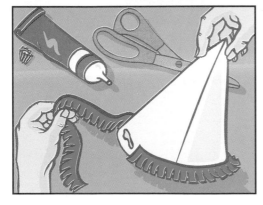

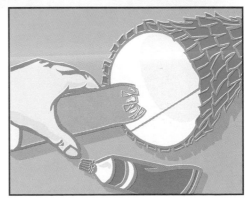

4. Glue a strip of crepe paper loosely around the bottom of the paper cone. Cut off the paper and glue down the end.

5. Glue more strips of crepe paper around the cone. Make sure each new strip just overlaps the one below it.

6. Make little cuts in one end of the cardboard roll. Press them inward. Cover them with glue and press them up into the cone.

POP-UP CARDS

Instead of buying cards to give your friends, why not make your own special cards? These pop-up cards are fun to make and are always a surprise when you open them. Try cutting out different shapes at the top of the cards to make monsters, ghosts, funny faces, or animals.

Things you need

Construction paper in different colors
Thin cardboard
Scissors and glue
Paints and felt-tip pens
Pencil

Paint and cut out a birthday cake. Fold it in half and put it inside your card.

Make a flower pop-up to give your mom on Mother's Day.

Slithery snake pop-up card

Witchy pop-up card

Witchy pop-up card

1. Fold a sheet of paper, 8 in. long and 4 in. wide, in half. Fold over the top corner, as shown. Fold it back and forth to make a crease.

2. Open the paper. Fold it in half, sideways, so that the bottom edge lines up with the top edge, as shown. Close the card, pulling out the fold.

3. Inside the card draw a witch shape where it pops out. Cut out the shape. Paint the card and write a message on the outside and on the inside.

Slithery snake card

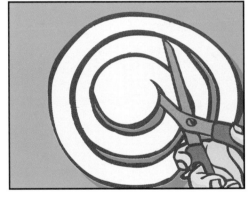

1. Fold a piece of thin cardboard, about 9½ in. by 4¾ in., in half. Press the fold down firmly. Cut out a piece of paper the same size as the folded card.

2. Cut off the corners of the piece of paper to make a neat circle. Cut the paper around and around from one edge toward the middle, as shown.

3. Paint the coil to look like a long, slithery snake. Cut out a forked tongue and glue it on. Glue the tail to the top of the card, as shown.

HANDY HINTS

When you fold the cardboard or paper, put the edges together so they meet exactly. Then the cards will look very neat.

To make cards that really pop out, fold them very carefully and press the folds down very hard to make good creases.

Decide what you want your card to look like before you start. You can get some very good ideas from picture books and magazines.

So that you don't make any mistakes, first draw the picture on a piece of paper and then copy it onto the cardboard or paper.

CRAZY CARDS

These crazy cards make good birthday and Christmas cards or party invitations. You can make them any size you like. If you have very big sheets of paper or cardboard, try making giant cards that will really surprise your friends.

Things you need

Thick paper or posterboard,
  both white and colored
Scissors and glue
Paints and felt-tip pens

HANDY HINTS

Use bright wrapping paper to make colorful strips for the busy cards.

Make a moving card that opens upward and pulls downward to open the door.

Open up a moving card so you can draw or paint a picture behind the door. Or cut out a picture from a magazine and glue it behind the door.

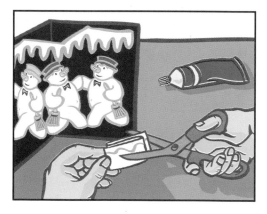

PULL

Be my valentine card

Busy cards

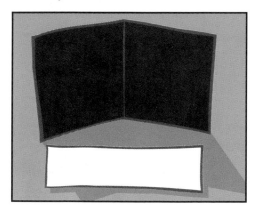

1. Cut a piece of posterboard the size you want your card to be and fold it in half. Cut a wide strip of paper slightly smaller than the card when it is opened up, as shown.

2. Fold the strip of paper in four equal parts. Draw a picture, like a snowman, on the front. Cut it out, leaving a link at each side. Open the paper. Paint the snowmen. Glue each end to the edge of the card.

3. Cut two narrow strips of paper. Fold them both in four equal parts. Draw a pattern on them and cut them out, leaving the links at each side. Glue the strips onto the top and bottom of the card.

Mother's Day card

Busy birthday card

Crazy Christmas card

Get-well card

PULL

Moving cards

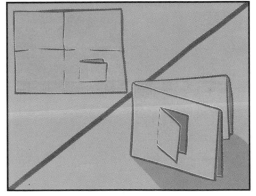

1. Fold a sheet of thick paper in half. Unfold it and fold it in half the other way. Open it out and cut a door in the bottom right square, as shown. Fold up the card.

2. Cut a strip of paper, almost as long as the open card. Cut two slits on the inside of the card, each a little longer than the width of the strip. Push the strip through the slits, as shown.

3. Glue the end of the strip to the edge of the door. Decorate the card. Write a message or draw a picture behind the door. Close the door. Write "PULL" on the end of the paper strip.

CLEVER COLLAGES

Collages are pictures and decorations made of cut-out or torn-out pictures and different kinds of paper. They make very good posters and calendars or party invitations. You can also use them to decorate cards and boxes, and to make pictures for presents. Photographs and advertisements from color magazines, vacation brochures, and some mail-order catalogs are all good for collages.

Things you need

Large sheets of paper or posterboard
Different kinds of colored paper, photographs, and advertisements
Glue and scissors
Pencil and ruler
Felt-tip pens and paints
Printed calendar
Ribbon

Silly picture

Calendar collage

1. Using a pencil and ruler, draw lines across a sheet of poster-board from the corners, as shown. Glue a calendar where the lines cross. This is the middle of the paper.

2. Tear strips of colored paper and glue them to the top and bottom of the posterboard. Cut out pictures; glue them around the calendar to make a scene, as shown. Let the glue dry.

3. Cut a piece of ribbon 2 in. long. Fold it in half, in a **V** shape. Glue the ends to the top of the back of the calendar to make a loop. When the glue is dry, hang up the calendar by the loop.

Spooky poster

Silly pictures

1. Draw lines with a pencil and ruler on a big sheet of paper. Write in the words you want on your spooky poster, spacing out the letters neatly. Fill them in with felt-tip pens or paint.

2. Cut out and glue colored pictures around the words. Choose spooky pictures to go with the theme. Glue the poster onto a piece of posterboard and tear around the edges.

Cut out a big photograph or advertisement and glue on lots of little pictures. Use photos of your family or of friends or animals, or just silly things to make a funny picture.

Collage calendar

Use different kinds of paper with odd textures, such as newspaper, tissue paper, or corrugated paper.

Spooky poster

PAPER WILDLIFE PARK

It is easy to make animals and birds out of thick paper, either colored or plain. Paint them carefully in realistic colors, or make them into strange, weird, and fantastic creatures. You can make wild animals and birds, or different kinds of farm animals.

Things you need

Stiff colored and plain paper
Scissors and glue
Pencil, paints, and felt-tip pens

Try using a small make-up sponge to decorate the paper animals with paint.

Make a weird and wonderful bird.

Glue a bushy tail onto a squirrel.

Tiger

Draw a tiger shape, as you did the giraffe's. Cut it out and paint it. Glue the sides of its head together, and then glue the tail.

Giraffe

Draw a giraffe's body on a piece of folded paper, with its back on the fold. Cut it out. Draw neck and head on stiff paper. Cut it out. Cut a slit in the backbone. Glue neck into it. Paint giraffe.

Elephant

Draw and cut out an elephant with its backbone along the fold of the paper. Glue on its trunk and then its tail. Cut two big ears. Glue them to the head. Paint the elephant.

Make trees in different shapes and sizes.

Give the lion a fringed paper mane.

Duck

Paper trees

Draw and cut out a duck's body as you did the giraffe's. Draw and cut out a head and neck. Glue the neck into a slit on the duck's backbone. Glue two wings to the body. Paint the duck.

1. Fold a sheet of stiff paper in half. With a pencil, draw the shape of a tree with a thick trunk, about 2 in. high. Cut out the tree shape.

2. Cut a slit up the trunk of one tree. Cut the other tree from the top to the trunk. Slot the two together, as shown. Glue them together along the slits.

31

PAPER PEOPLE

These two pages show you how to make paper people in lots of different shapes and sizes. Try making a family of paper people, a clown, a strange magician, an angel, or a nasty monster. You can glue on paper eyes and mouths, paper hair, horns, big ears, some scary paper teeth, a beard, or a curly mustache.

Things you need

Cardboard tubes from
  toilet paper, paper towel,
  or tinfoil rolls
Plain and colored paper
Paper towels
Cardboard
Glue, scissors, tape, and a
  pencil
Paints or felt-tip pens
Newspaper

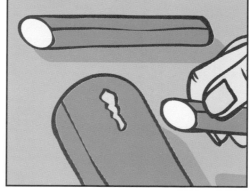

Give the magician an exotic hat, cape, and beard.

Paint the clown's clothes or decorate them with paper shapes.

Clown

1. To make the clown's legs, make a groove with scissors halfway down a long cardboard tube. Glue colored paper around the legs. Glue a different color around the top half of the tube.

2. For the arms, cut out two pieces of stiff paper, 5 in. long and 2 in. wide. Roll each piece into a tube and glue the edges. Cut one end of each arm at an angle and glue it onto the tube.

3. To make the clown's head, scrunch up some newspaper into a ball. Then wrap a paper towel around it. Push the neck into the top of the tube and tape it in place. Glue on cardboard feet.

Dumpies

1. For the body and head, wrap two pieces of paper around a short cardboard tube. Glue down the edges. Cut out cardboard feet and glue them onto the end of the tube, as shown.

2. Fold a piece of stiff paper in half. Draw an arm and hand shape and cut it out. Glue an arm to each side of the body. For hair, make lots of cuts in a strip of thin paper. Glue it on.

3. To make a hat, cut out a small circle of paper. Make one cut to the middle of the circle, as shown. Overlap the edges and glue them down. Glue the hat on the top of the Dumpy.

Decorate the Dumpies' clothes with paper shapes.

You can use gift-wrapping ribbon to make an angel with shiny paper hair.

HANDY HINTS

If you don't have any cardboard tubes, roll a piece of thin cardboard into a tube and glue or tape down the edge.

To make a tall cone, roll up a sheet of paper. Make one end pointed and the other end wide. Glue down the edge of the paper. Cut off the top and bottom to make neat edges.

HANDSOME HATS

You can make all sorts of different paper hats to wear at parties or just for fun. Ask your friends to come to a fancy hat party wearing their own crazy paper hats. The person with the best hat can win a prize.

Things you need

Posterboard or large sheets of
   construction paper in different
   colors
Gold and silver paper
Scissors, pencil, and glue
Paints or felt-tip pens
Small colorful candies

To make a cap, cut out a bill of stiff paper and glue it onto a round hat that does not have a brim.

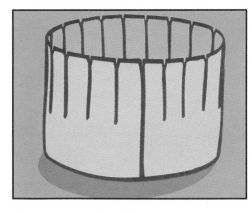

Use a black felt-tip pen to decorate the cotton wool on your crown. Then it will look like real ermine.

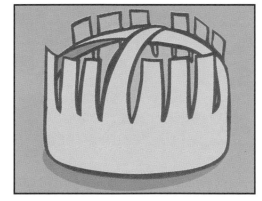

For a clown's hat, cut out different-colored paper dots and stick them onto a tall cone hat. Stick shapes around the bottom.

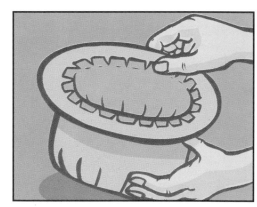

Round hat

1. Cut a strip of paper, about 10 in. wide and long enough to go around your head. Cut slits, about halfway down, all along the strip. Glue the ends of the strip together, as shown.

2. Bend over a strip on each side and glue the ends together in the middle. Glue two strips from the two other sides in the middle. Glue together, one pair at a time, all the other strips.

3. Put the hat down on a sheet of paper. Carefully draw around it. Cut out the circle and a wider one around it for the brim. Cut small slits around the bottom of the hat. Glue them to the brim.

If you do not have a sheet of paper big enough to go around your head, glue the edges of two sheets together.

Crowns for kings and queens look best made out of gold or silver paper. Glue strips of tinfoil to a strip of paper to make a sparkling silver crown.

Make a witch's hat out of black paper. Glue on spooky shapes.

Roll strips of tinfoil into little wheels to glue onto a crown.

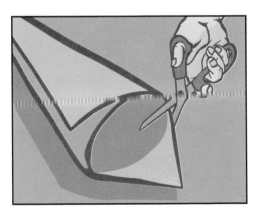

Crazy crown

Cone hat

1. Cut a strip of gold paper, about 6 in. wide and long enough to go around your head. Fold it in three but do not crease the edges. Draw a crown shape, as shown, and then cut it out.

2. Unfold the paper and glue the ends together. Cut out jewel shapes from shiny paper. Glue them around the crown. You can also glue on small colorful candies as jewels.

Cut a piece of paper, 1 ft. wide and long enough to go around your head. Roll it into a cone, and glue the edges. Cut off the extra paper. Paint the hat, or cut out shapes and glue them onto it.

MARVELOUS MASKS

Masks are fun to wear at costume parties or on special occasions like Halloween. Make some for your friends, or choose a theme such as animal, alien, or spooky masks and ask them to make their own. Once you have made the base, you can add things like hair, eyelashes, feathers, or whiskers. You can make small eye masks or whole face masks.

Make a space mask out of silver paper. Glue on tinfoil and other space-age objects.

Things you need

Sheets of thick plain and
  colored paper
Colored paper to decorate
  your mask
Thin rolled elastic
Big needle
Glue, scissors, and tape
Pencil

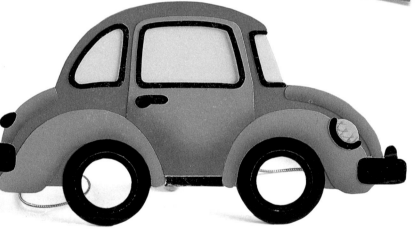

Draw and paint a car, like this Beetle, on stiff cardboard. Cut out the middle of the wheels as eye holes. Fasten on elastic for the headband.

Crafty cat mask

1. Draw this mask shape on a sheet of thick paper. Make it about 2¼ in. deep and 4¾ in. wide. Cut it out. Cut out two eye holes in the middle of the mask, about 1 in. apart.

2. Cut two small ear shapes out of pink paper. Glue one to the inside of each ear. Cut out whiskers and a nose. Then glue them onto the mask.

3. Add more decorations. Then wrap a length of elastic around your head and cut it to fit. Thread it through a needle and through the mask, as shown. Knot each end at the holes in the mask.

To be sure that a mask will fit you, hold a sheet of paper against your face and mark where your eyes are with a pencil. Then carefully cut out the eye holes.

Instead of decorating your mask with paper shapes, you can paint it with poster paints. The paint may make the paper a little bit floppy. Let it dry and it will stiffen again.

To make a really jazzy mask, glue on sequins feathers, sparkles, beads or buttons.

Crazy face mask

1. Draw a face, about 8 in. high and 4¾ in. wide, on some paper. Draw two eyes, 1 in. apart, a nose, and a mouth. Cut out the face. Cut out the eye holes and a flap for the nose.

2. Fold a second sheet of paper. Cut out two ears. Tape one to each side of the face. Cut out decorations, such as bright paper flowers and dangling earrings, to glue or tape on your mask.

3. To make a really crazy face, glue on paper eyelashes, spiky hair, and red lips. Measure a piece of elastic around your head. Thread it through a needle and knot it onto the mask.

PRETTY PLATES

You can make wonderful plates and bowls in many different shapes using old newspapers, flour, and water. Brightly painted and varnished, they make beautiful decorations and good presents. Instead of painting them, try covering your plates with colorful tissue paper or pictures cut out of magazines.

Things you need

Old newspapers
Flour and water
Bowl for mixing and a tablespoon
Plastic wrap or petroleum jelly
Old plate or bowl
Poster paints and a paintbrush
Scissors and water-based varnish

Painted plate

Tissue-paper plate

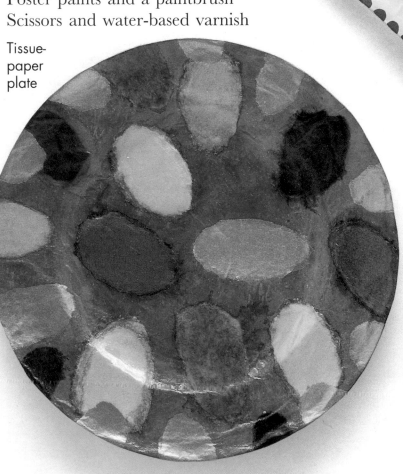

HANDY HINTS

Try using different-shaped plates and bowls. But don't use ones that slope inward at the top or you won't be able to take your paper plate or bowl off when it is finished.

Rest the plate on a small bowl to keep it away from the tabletop so that you can easily glue bits of newspaper around the edge.

Instead of using flour and water, you can use ordinary wallpaper paste.

Painted paper plate

1. To make the paste, put two tablespoons of flour in a bowl and add four or five tablespoons of cold water. Stir it well until it is like thin cream. Add more water if it is too thick.

2. Hold four pages of newspaper together and tear them into strips, about 1 in. wide. Then tear the strips into little squares, about the size of large postage stamps, as shown.

3. Cover a plate with plastic wrap to keep the paper from sticking. Wrap it tightly and smooth down all the folds. Instead of plastic wrap you can cover the plate with petroleum jelly.

4. Brush a layer of flour paste onto the plate. Cover it with a layer of newspaper squares, over-lapping the edges. Brush on more paste. Put on a second layer of newspaper. Let it dry.

5. Repeat step 4 until you have five or six layers. Let the newspaper dry completely. When it is dry, cut around the plate or bowl with scissors to make a nice neat edge.

6. Carefully take off the dried paper from the plate or bowl. Then remove the plastic wrap. Paint the paper plate with poster paints. When it is dry, brush on varnish and let it dry again.

Cover a bowl with pictures cut out of a magazine.

Paint a bowl on the inside as well as the outside. Use it to hold fruit or paper flowers.

39

FANCY LANTERNS

Paper lanterns look good as party decorations or just to decorate your room. You can make them in different colors and paint on extra designs. Glitter paint makes them sparkle. Make them any size you like and hang them up on their own or in a row. Just be sure not to put light bulbs or candles inside of them.

To make them even fancier, paint different patterns on your lanterns.

Things you need

Construction paper in different colors
Very thin colored paper
Big and small plates
Scissors and glue
Pencil
Poster paints, glitter paint, and a paintbrush

A really big lantern looks good hanging from the ceiling.

Fancy lantern

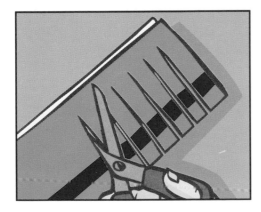

1. Fold a sheet of construction paper in half, lengthwise. Crease it down the middle. Make deep cuts all the way along the folded edge.

2. Unfold the paper. Spread glue along the two short edges, as shown. Bend the paper around and press the edges together until they are firmly glued.

3. Cut a narrow strip of paper for the handle. Glue each end to the top of the lantern, on the inside. Let it dry before you hang up the lantern.

Make lots of little lanterns in different colors and hang them on a string.

Glue on strips of colored or metallic paper.

HANDY HINTS

If you want to make lots of little lanterns, fold up several sheets of paper together and cut them at the same time.

When you hang up the lacy lantern, it will slowly drop down and open up. If the lower part doesn't open, slip a coin into it. The weight will pull it down.

Paint a lantern while it is flat and before you cut it and glue it together.

Lacy lantern

1. Put two sheets of very thin paper on top of each other. Put a plate down on top of them and draw a circle around it. Cut out the circles and pull them apart.

2. Fold one circle in half, then in half again, and again. Make cuts along both edges, as shown. Do the same to the second circle. Open both circles.

3. Carefully glue the two circles together at the edges. Cut out a strip of paper for the handle. Glue the ends to the middle of one circle. Let the glue dry.

DAZZLING DECORATIONS

Use shiny paper in bright colors to make these dazzling decorations. Make little ones to hang on the Christmas tree. Or light up a room with rows of golden angels, silver bells, and sparkling paper chains.

Things you need

Shiny wrapping paper, including gold and silver
Thin paper in bright colors
Scissors and glue
Plate and cup

Hang chains, bells, and angels across a room.

Use two different colors to make the lacy balls.

Lacy balls

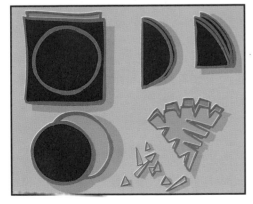

1. Put two sheets of paper on top of each other. Draw a circle around a cup on the paper. Cut it out. Fold each circle of paper in half, in half again, and again. Snip bits out of the sides.

2. Unfold the two circles. Fold each one in half. Tape or glue them together at the folds. Glue on a thin paper handle as shown. Space out the four sides of the lacy ball.

HANDY HINTS

To make chains really quickly, fold up a big sheet of paper so that you can cut out lots of strips at the same time.

To make decorations of different sizes, try using different-sized plates or cups to draw around.

Instead of using thin paper to make the lacy balls, you can use tissue paper.

42

Bright bells

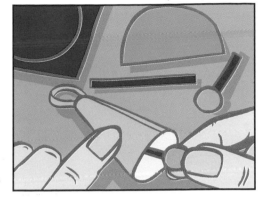

To make a cone, draw around a plate on a piece of paper. Cut out the circle. Cut it in half. Roll half into a cone; glue the edges. Glue on a paper handle and ringer.

Golden angel

Make a cone out of shiny gold paper. Draw a wing shape, as shown, on a folded piece of paper. Cut it out. Glue the wings to the cone. Then glue on a head and a thin handle.

Candy cone

Make a cone and turn it upside down. Cut a thin paper handle and glue it on, as shown. When the glue is dry, fill the cone with little candies, cookies, or very small presents.

Sparkling chains

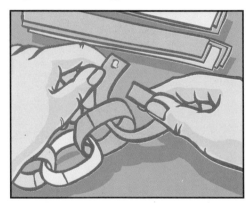

Cut out strips of shiny paper, about 8 in. long and 1 in. wide. Glue the ends of a strip together. Loop a second strip through it and glue the ends. Add more strips to make a long chain.

Hang the candy cones up on a ribbon.

Glue paper eyes, a mouth, and a halo on the angel's face.

PERFECT PAPER FRUIT

Paper fruit is easy to make and looks like real fruit! Try making different kinds of fruit, such as apples, bananas, pears, or oranges, any size you like. They look good in a bowl, as a table decoration, or hanging from an indoor plant or tree.

Things you need

Old newspaper
Plain paper
White flour and a
  tablespoon
Bowl for mixing
Plastic wrap
Scissors and glue
Poster paints and
  a paintbrush
Pencil

Round orange

Red and green apples

A perfect pear

Paper apple

1. Put one tablespoon of flour in the bowl. Add three or four tablespoons of water. Stir it well until it is like thin cream without any lumps in it.

2. Tear a sheet of newspaper into long strips, about 1 in. wide. Tear the long strips into small squares, about the size of large postage stamps.

3. Scrunch up two sheets of newspaper very tightly into a ball or the shape you want the fruit to be. Put plastic wrap around it to help it keep its shape.

44

Purple plums

Lovely lemon

HANDY HINTS

To make shiny, beautiful fruit that lasts longer, brush on a layer of water-based varnish.

Smooth down the newspaper squares with your fingers to get a smooth, round shape.

Instead of using plastic wrap, you can wrap masking tape around the fruit.

To make your fruit look like real fruit, dab on the paint with a tiny sponge.

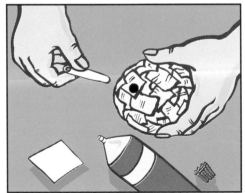

Big banana

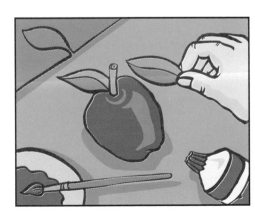

4. Brush paste over the fruit shape. Cover it with newspaper squares, making sure they all overlap. Brush on more paste. Put on a second layer of paper.

5. For a stalk, cut out a small square of white paper. Roll it up. Glue down the edge. Make a hole with a pencil in the top of the fruit and stick the stalk in.

6. Let the fruit dry for at least one day. Then paint it all over with a thick layer of paint. Cut out paper leaves and glue them to the stalk.

MADCAP MOBILES

Make this spooky mobile, or design your own special mobile to hang up from a lampshade or any high place in a room. Mobiles make good presents to give to young children and babies to decorate their bedrooms. They love to watch them slowly twist and turn as they lie in bed.

Things you need

Colored drinking straws
Construction paper in different colors
Glow-in-the-dark paper or pens
Strong thread and a big needle
Tape, pencil, and scissors
Paints or felt-tip pens

HANDY HINTS

If a mobile does not hang level, slide the thread along a straw a little. Move it until the straws hang right.

Make a zany space mobile.

Spooky mobile

1. Put the ends of two straws together. They must be exactly the same size and length. Wind tape around them to make a long straw. Make two more long straws in the same way.

2. Draw seven spooky shapes, such as a bat, ghost, skeleton, pumpkin, or wicked witch, on construction paper. They should all be about the same size. Cut them out.

3. Put the middles of the three long straws across each other. Tape them together, one at a time, as shown. Make sure that the space between each one is the same.

Tie on more straws, threads, and shapes to make a very busy mobile.

Fishy mobile

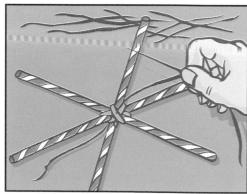

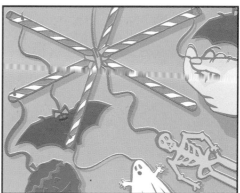

4. Cut eight pieces of thread, each about 20 in. long. Thread one through the needle. Push the needle through the middle of the straws, as shown. Tie the thread in a knot around them.

5. Paint or color the seven spooky shapes. Give them long, sharp teeth, scary faces, or black clothes. Glue on bits of glow-in-the-dark paper for the eyes and mouths. Let them dry.

6. Stick one end of a thread through the top of each monster. Stick the other ends through the straws and one from the center. Knot the thread ends. Hang the mobile by the middle thread.

FABULOUS FOLDERS

Folders are very useful for keeping letters, secret papers, and all kinds of odds and ends in. They also make very good presents for your friends and family. You can decorate them with drawings or paintings, or glue on cut-out pictures or patterns made from colored paper.

Things you need

Plain or colored posterboard
Glue, scissors, and
  paper-fasteners
Ribbon and string
Pencil and ruler
Large coin

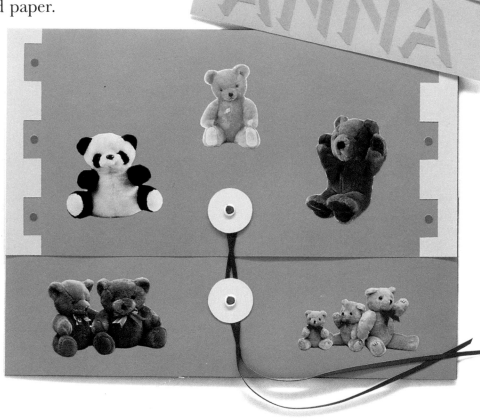

Decorate your folder with pictures and patterns cut out of magazines or made from colored paper.

Fancy folder

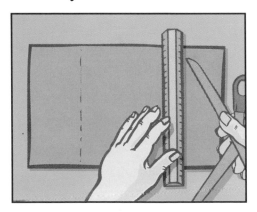

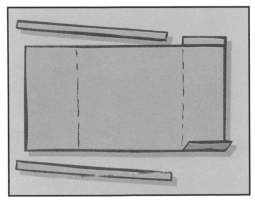

1. Cut out a piece of posterboard, about 20 in. long and 13 in. wide. Measure 6 in. from one edge and make a groove with scissors, as shown. Measure 5 in. from the other edge. Make another groove there.

2. Measure ½ in. along the top and bottom edges. Draw two lines. Cut off the strips to the second groove. Fold the posterboard along the lines. Fold over the strips and press along the creases, as shown.

3. Cut a small slit at each end of the posterboard, as shown. Cut two pieces of ribbon, 12 in. long. Push the end of one ribbon through a slit. Glue down the end. Then glue on the other ribbon.

48

Folder with fasteners

1. Draw two circles around a large coin on posterboard. Cut out the circles. Make a small hole in the middle of each circle with scissors. Push a paper-fastener into each hole.

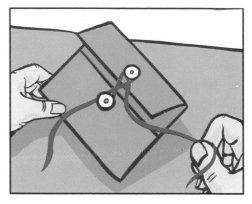

2. Push each fastener into the folder near the edges and press down the prongs. Wind some string, 8 in. long, around one fastener, under one circle, and then around the other.

Paint on a friend's name and give the folder away as a present.

HANDY HINTS

You can make folders of any size. All you need is a piece of posterboard about twice as long as it is wide.

When you fold up a folder along the grooves, press the closed scissors along the lines to make a good crease.

4. Fold up the strips on the top and bottom of the posterboard. Fold up the right-hand side of the posterboard and glue down the strips. Close the folder and tie the ribbons in a neat bow.

Give everyone in your secret club his or her own special folder.

CLEVER CARDBOARD CLOCKS

You can use all sorts of cardboard boxes to make interesting clocks. This is a simple one but you can invent your own shapes. Use one to teach a small child how to tell time. Or make a clock each for your mom and dad. They can use them to tell each other what time they are going out or when they will be home.

Things you need

Small cardboard boxes
Plain and colored paper
Thin cardboard
Pins or very small nails
Glue, scissors, and tape
Poster paints or felt-tip pens
Cup or small jar

To make an elegant clock, glue on pieces of metallic paper.

Glue on funny hands and feet.

Clever clock

1. Shut the lid of a small, sturdy, rectangular cardboard box. Tape down the lid and the open sides with strong tape. Then neatly snip off any extra pieces of tape, as shown.

2. Cut a piece of thin cardboard the same width as the sides of the box and twice as long as the top. Fold the cardboard in half and tape it to the sides of the box to make a roof, as shown.

3. Cut two small pieces of thin cardboard and tape them to the front and back of the box. Cut off the extra cardboard at the top, as shown. Tape down the edges of the roof.

Make different-
shaped hands like
these fishy ones.

Paint Roman
numerals on a
castle clock.

Wrap paper around
a box very tightly.
Crease the edges with
your fingers to make
a neat finish.

When you write the
numbers on the clock
face, start with 12 at
the top. Write in 6 at
the bottom and 3 and
9 on the sides. Then
neatly fill in the rest of
the numbers.

Look at lots of clocks
and watches to see
the different kinds of
numbers used.

Use small scissors to
cut out the hands for a
little clock.

Paint bright
numbers
all over
your
clock.

4. Wrap the box in a sheet of paper. Glue it on. Cut off the extra pieces around the roof, as shown. Glue down the paper on the roof.

5. Draw a circle around a cup or small jar on a sheet of paper. Cut it out. Write the numbers 1 to 12 neatly around the circle to look like a clock. Glue the circle to the front of the box.

6. For the hands, draw one big and one small arrow on some thin cardboard. Cut them out. Push a pin through both hands. Then push the pin through the middle of the clock face.

51

FUN WITH
PAINT

• MOIRA BUTTERFIELD •

MATERIALS, TIPS, AND HINTS

In this section there are lots of different painting projects for you to try. You can probably find most of the things you need for them around the house, but some may have to be bought from a craft or art supply store. As well as simple step-by-step directions for every project, there are Handy Hints to help you.

For most painting you need poster or tempera paints or watercolors, but a few projects need special kinds of paint, such as acrylics or oils. You will also need fat and thin paintbrushes and special brushes for stenciling.

Powdered poster paint needs to be mixed with water.

Poster paint is water-based and washes off easily. It is the cheapest kind of paint to buy.

Ready-mixed poster paint is sold in jars. You can buy big jars and pour out a little at a time.

You can also buy poster paint in small, hard blocks, which you mix with water.

Oil paints are the most expensive. They come in small tubes and aren't mixed with water.

Brushes, paper, and pots

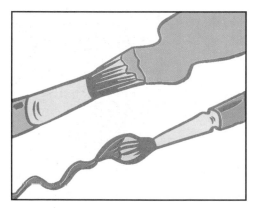

1. Some brushes have flat ends and some have pointed ends. Flat ends are good for painting backgrounds. Pointed brushes are good for painting thin lines.

2. Some brushes have soft bristles and some have much harder, pricklier bristles. It is best to try out different kinds of brushes for different projects.

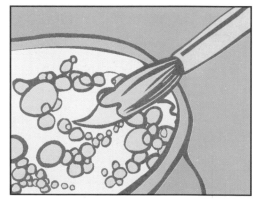

3. Always wash your brushes in soapy water when you have finished using them. Otherwise they will dry stiff, and the bristles will stick together.

Acrylic paints don't wash off easily. They are thick, bright, and usually sold in tubes or plastic jars.

HANDY HINTS

Painting can be a very messy business. It's a good idea to wear an old shirt or apron to keep you clean. Cover your work surface with old newspaper and put a couple of plastic garbage bags on the floor, underneath the table.

It's best to paint in a room where there is a sink close by, so that you can keep changing your paint water.

Keep an eye out for things that might be useful, such as plastic containers, tinfoil, old toothbrushes, cardboard, or old sponges.

Watercolor paints are quite expensive. They come in small tubes or blocks, which are then mixed with water. It is best to use them on white paper.

4. You will need some small cups for water. Old yogurt containers are ideal. An old baking tray makes a very good palette to mix your paints on.

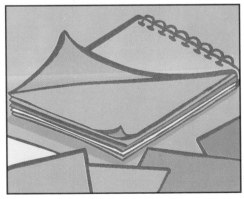

5. If you use paper that is too thin, the paint will make it crinkle up when it dries. Thick watercolor paper is best. It is cheapest if you buy a pad.

6. Strong glue or paste works best on cardboard. Glue sticks are clean and easy to use for gluing lightweight paper.

MIXING COLORS

On these two pages you can find out how to mix paints together to make all sorts of different colors. All you really need are five main colors — yellow, red, blue, black, and white — to make all the colors on the opposite page. Before you start the projects in this book, experiment to see how many colors you can create.

HANDY HINTS

When you have loaded your brush with paint, do not dip it into another color. Otherwise you will make your paints muddy.

Change the water you use as soon as it gets dirty, so that you have nice clean colors to paint with.

If you put the paint on thickly, the color will be dark and rich. The more water you mix into the paint, the more delicate the color will look.

Experiments with color

1. A light color looks brightest against a dark backgound. Try putting white paint on black paper and see how strong the white paint looks.

2. You can make many different shades from one color, depending on how thick or thin the paint is. Try painting a whole picture with just one color.

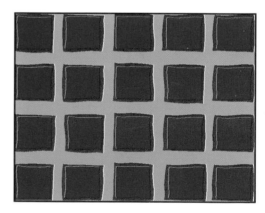

3. Pastel shades are colors that are mixed with white. Pale pink, pale blue, and pale yellow are all pastel shades. Try making your own pastel colors.

4. When you paint a picture on white paper, leave some of the white showing. It may help to make your painting look fresher and cleaner.

5. Experiment by painting rows of patterns, using two or three colors, as shown. Then you can easily see which colors you like using together best.

6. Some colors clash with each other, such as red and pink, green or orange. But you can use them together to get a really bright and jazzy effect.

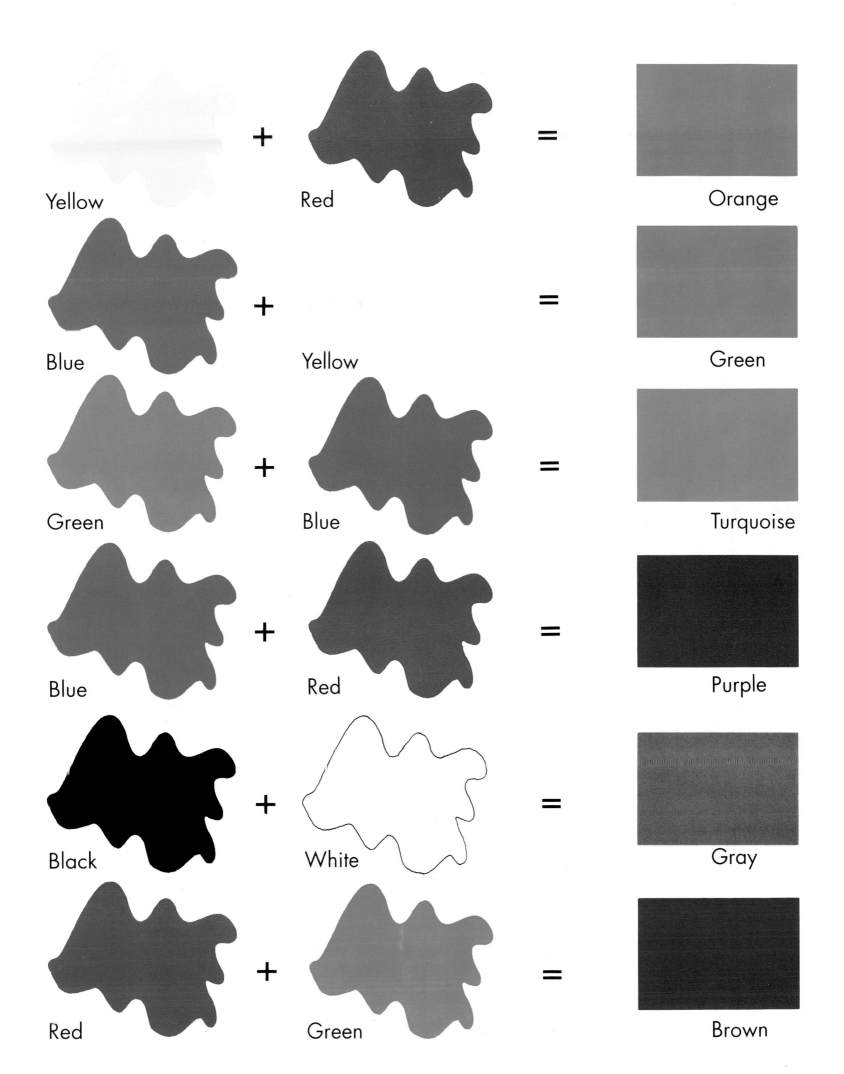

Yellow + Red = Orange

Blue + Yellow = Green

Green + Blue = Turquoise

Blue + Red = Purple

Black + White = Gray

Red + Green = Brown

COMBING AND BRUSHING

You can get all sorts of different patterns and pictures by dragging a comb or a stiff brush across thickly painted paper. Try making your own combs out of thick cardboard, with either blunt teeth or sharp teeth, to use as scrapers.

Things you need

Colored paper
Thin and thick cardboard
Poster paints, including
   gold and silver
Paintbrushes and palette
Plastic comb
Old hairbrush
Crepe paper and
   scissors
Thin ribbon

Draw a coiled-up snake. Paint it and comb patterns in it. Cut out the snake and hang it up.

Golden gift tag

HANDY HINTS

To cover the teeth of a comb or the bristles of a toothbrush with paint, it is easiest to brush the paint on with an ordinary paintbrush.

Try putting blobs of paint onto paper and then dragging it into swirls with a comb.

Golden gift tag

  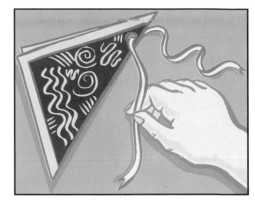

1. Paint a square of paper, about 4 in. by 4 in., with thick, gold poster paint. Make sure the paint covers the paper completely. Leave it to dry.

2. Now paint a layer of black paint on top of the gold paint. While this is wet, run the teeth of a comb across it, pressing down to make different patterns.

3. When the paint is dry, fold the square in half, diagonally. Poke a hole in one corner and thread thin ribbon through it.

Perfect party chains

Perfect party chains

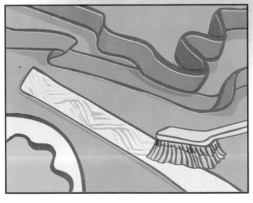  

1. Cut two long strips of crepe paper. Cover the teeth of a comb or bristles of a hairbrush with paint. Brush or dot them onto the strips.

2. Let the paint dry, then decorate the other side. When they're dry again, lay the strips at right angles and overlap them, as shown. Tape the ends.

3. Pull out the finished chain to use as a party decoration. You can decorate red and green crepe paper to make perfect Christmas decorations.

STRAW AND SPLATTER PAINTINGS

You can have great fun making all sorts of splotchy paintings using straws, toothbrushes, or nailbrushes. Use colored paper as well as white to make some interesting patterns. It is best to wear an apron and cover the floor or table with newspaper, as this can be a bit messy.

Things you need

Poster paints and palette
Sheets of white and colored paper
Drinking straws, old toothbrush,
  nailbrush, and paintbrushes
Water and newspaper

HANDY HINTS

Practice putting lots of colors together when putting on paint and see the strange effects.

Cut out different cardboard shapes (stencils) and lay them on the paper before you splatter it with paint. They will leave clear shapes on your picture.

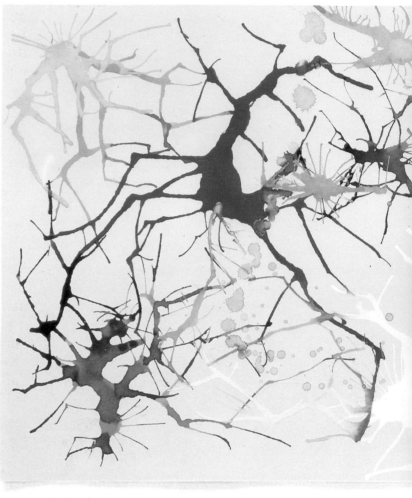

Splotchy straw painting

Blowing with straws

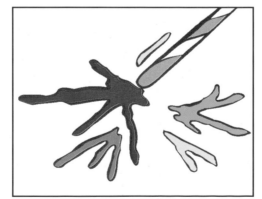

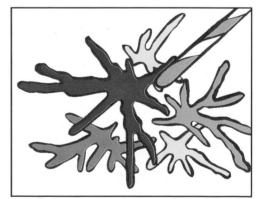

1. Mix your paints with plenty of water to make them runny. Splatter some paint onto your paper with a paintbrush, or paint on runny lines.

2. Blow the runny paint all over the page using a drinking straw. Dab some extra water onto the paper if the paint is not quite runny enough.

3. Gradually splatter on more colors. If you do this while the paint is wet, the different colors will mix together as you blow them around the paper.

Splatter paint through a stencil to make these pictures.

Dab thick paint on paper with the end of a straw to make apple trees.

Lost in space

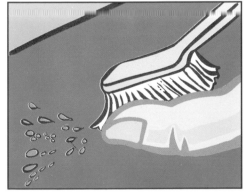

1. To make a starry sky, dab an old toothbrush into white or orange paint. Hold it over a sheet of dark blue or black paper with the bristles facing down.

2. Gently run your finger along the bristles toward you to spray the paint over the paper. (If you do it the other way, you will get sprayed with paint!)

3. Flick paint onto the sky with a paintbrush to make bigger stars. Add a moon, shooting stars, and rockets.

SEEING DOUBLE

The mirror prints on these two pages are quick and easy to make, and every one is different. They are called mirror prints because the pictures on both sides of the folded paper are exactly the same, like the reflection in a mirror. One of the best ways to do them is by using string dipped in paint. The string makes all sorts of swirling patterns on the paper.

Things you need

Sheets of paper, string, and poster paints
Old saucers, paintbrush, and stirrer

Swirling string pictures

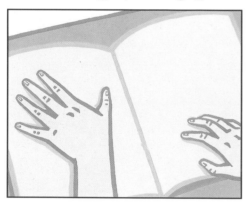

1. Fold a big sheet of white or colored paper in half. Then smooth it out again, as shown.

2. Cut two or three short lengths of string. Then put two or three different-colored thick poster paints in old saucers.

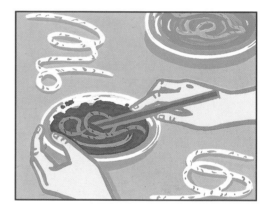

3. Stir each piece of string into a different color, as shown. Make sure that they are all completely covered with poster paint.

4. Put the strings down on one side of the paper. Arrange them any way you like, with the ends poking out over one edge.

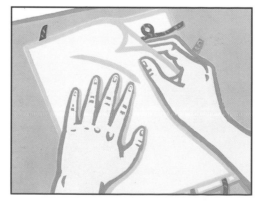

5. Fold the paper in half again on top of the coils of painted string. Then gently smooth it down with your hand, as shown.

6. Hold the paper down with one hand and pull out the strings, one by one, by the ends. Very carefully unfold the paper.

Paint a person on one side and fold the paper over to make these two terrible twins.

To make two fighting monsters, paint a fierce monster facing the middle. Then fold the paper over.

Paint one half of a butterfly, then fold the paper over.

Paint half a castle and then fold over the paper.

Swirling string picture

63

WAYS WITH WAX

Crayons are made of wax, which is waterproof and does not mix with paint. But if you paint over crayon with one or two layers of thick paint you can make some unusual pictures and patterns. Use lots of crayons and try scratching out a peacock or landscape scene.

Things you need

Crayons
Tempera, poster, or watercolor
  paints
Thick paintbrush
Thick paper
Small scissors or knitting
  needle

This beautiful peacock has been scratched through black poster paint.

Wax and scratch

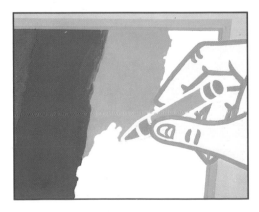

1. Draw thick bands with different-colored crayons on a sheet of paper. Press down hard with the crayons.

2. Paint over the bands of crayon with thick, black poster paint until they are covered with paint. Let the paint dry.

3. Using a knitting needle or scissors, scratch a picture through the paint. The crayon will show through.

HANDY HINTS

Wax shows up best through thinly painted watercolors.

It's easiest to draw your picture first with a pencil. It won't show up when you go over it with crayon.

Use watercolor paint on wax to make patterned picture frames.

Framed wax-on-wax pictures

Wax on wax

1. To make a scratch picture without paint, cover the paper with a light-colored crayon in an oval, as shown.

2. Cover the pale color with a darker one. When you scratch out a picture the pale color will show through.

3. Cut out an oval frame from cardboard for your picture. Decorate the frame with crayons and paint over it with thin paint.

PAINTING WITH ODDS AND ENDS

You don't always need a paintbrush to paint a picture. You can get very strange and interesting effects by dabbing a sponge, cloth, or scrunched-up paper into paint and then pressing it onto paper. Here are some ways to make special paint patterns.

Things you need

Poster paints, old newspaper, and a plate
Tissue paper and empty chip bag
Corrugated paper and waffle-weave dish towel

HANDY HINTS

You can use paper, a sponge, plastic bubble wrap, or a textured cloth to make different paint patterns. Look for things around the house to make your own special paint effects.

When you have practiced making patterns, you can use them to paint interesting pictures and Christmas or birthday cards, like the ones below.

Make cards, gift tags, and pictures out of paintings.

Tissue-paper flowers

1. Cut a circle out of tissue paper. Poke the middle of the circle down between your thumb and forefinger to make a paper rosette, as shown.

2. Mix some poster paint on an old plate. Hold onto the underneath of the rosette, as shown, and dab the top gently into the paint.

3. Press the rosette gently onto a piece of paper. When you lift it up, there will be a flower shape. Do this again or use different-sized circles to make more flowers.

Plastic bag snowstorm

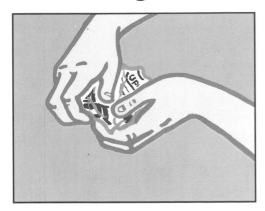

1. Scrunch up some stiff plastic into a ball. An empty chip bag is best. (A plastic sandwich bag may be too soft.)

2. Mix white poster paint on an old plate. Then dab the ball of scrunched-up plastic gently into the paint.

3. Dab the ball onto a piece of blue paper, as shown, to make a pattern that looks like falling snow.

More patterns to make

For patterned lines, use the edge of a piece of corrugated cardboard.

For a net pattern, use a woven-string dishcloth.

To make swirls, move a scrunched-up ball of paper from side to side.

67

CARDBOARD CREATIONS

These amazing models are all made with things that you can easily find around the house, such as cardboard tubes, egg cartons, milk cartons, and empty juice cans. Once you have made them, you can paint them with poster paints.

Things you need for the jolly giraffe

5 small cardboard tubes (toilet paper rolls are ideal)
Paper towel roll
Egg carton
Corrugated cardboard
String and strong glue
Tape and scissors
Poster paints

Make a totem pole out of cardboard rolls stuck together and painted. Decorate it with bits of cards.

Make this strange egg carton alien out of an empty egg carton with a cardboard roll mouth and antennae, cardboard tongue, and tinfoil hair.

Jolly giraffe

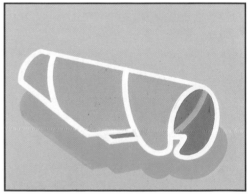

1. Using strong glue, stick a toilet paper roll onto each corner of the egg carton. These are the giraffe's legs and body. Let the glue dry.

2. To make the neck, cut slits in one end of the paper towel roll and bend them out. Stick the roll onto the egg carton and then tape it down firmly.

3. For the giraffe's head, cut a toilet paper roll into the shape shown above. Glue it on the neck and tape it firmly in place.

HANDY HINTS

You can glue things like yarn, cotton balls, foil, and pieces of foam onto your models, and then paint over them.

You may need to paint more than one layer of paint on your model to cover it. Make sure each layer dries before you paint the next one.

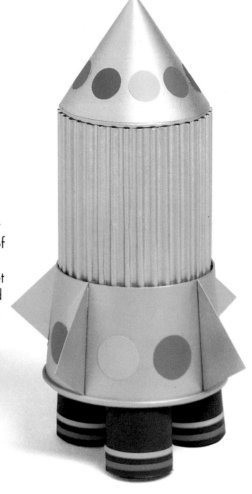

Make this super spaceship out of ice cream containers, toilet paper rolls, and thin cardboard.

Jolly giraffe

4. For the giraffe's mane, glue a long, thin piece of corrugated cardboard down the back of the neck. Glue on a string tail and fray the end, as shown.

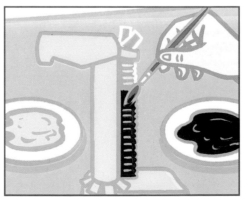

5. Paint the giraffe's body with poster paint. Let it dry and paint on a second coat. Paint the mane and tail. Let them dry.

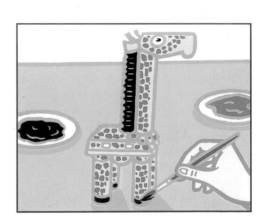

6. When the paint is dry, paint spots all over the giraffe's body. Add eyes and a mouth and hooves, as shown.

PAINT PRINTS

You can make striking pictures and wild patterns by printing with leaves, string, vegetables, and even cookies. The secret of making good prints is to use paint that is sticky, not wet. Here are some ideas for printing shapes on paper and fabric.

Things you need

Poster paint
Old tray
Sponge (for a printing pad)
Paintbrush and plain paper
Different-shaped shiny leaves,
  carrots, potatoes, and cookies
Paring knife (Have a parent help.)

Vegetable print writing
paper and envelopes

Making a print pad

1. Mix paint with a little water, keeping the paint thick and sticky. Put a sponge inside a tray and pour the paint over the sponge.

2. Press vegetable shapes or leaves onto the sponge to cover them with paint. Then press them onto paper. Rinse out the sponge to change the color.

Vegetable prints

1. Cut a carrot in half. Cut one end, leaving a raised shape, as shown. Cut a different shape out of one end of the other half.

2. Cut a potato in half and pat it dry. Cut one end, leaving a raised shape and use it to print patterns. You can decorate writing paper, envelopes, and fabric.

70

To print on fabric you need special fabric paints. Make sure you put a sheet of newspaper under your work when you start printing.

If you have put too much paint on your printing shape, dab it on newspaper first to make the paint less thick.

Vegetable print moon and stars

Falling leaves

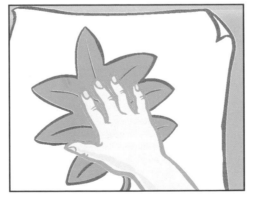

1. Collect leaves with a shiny, waxy surface that are nice and strong. Brush paint on the leaf or use a printing pad.

2. Carefully put the painted leaf, facedown, on a piece of plain paper. Press it down gently with your fingers, as shown.

3. Gently peel off the leaf. It will leave a print behind. Make prints with the same leaf in different colors, or try using different leaves.

SNAPPY STENCILS

Stenciling makes the same picture or pattern over and over again by painting through (or around) a piece of cardboard. You can stencil on paper, fabric, or wood. It's best to practice with an easy shape when you start. Once you have gotten used to stenciling, try some more interesting and complicated ideas.

Things you need

Stiff cardboard
Watercolor paper
Small scissors or
　craft knife
Thick paint
Stencil brush or
　paintbrush with
　stiff bristles
Natural sponge

Cut-out clown stencil

Cut-out clown

1. Fold a piece of cardboard in half. Draw one half of the clown along the fold line, as shown. Cut around the clown shape and then open the card.

2. Hold the stencil firmly on the paper with one hand. Then dab the paint inside the clown shape, using a special stencil brush.

3. You can use different colors for different parts of the clown. Make sure you allow each color to dry before taking the stencil card away.

Make a border by repeating the stencil pattern many times.

Stencil pattern

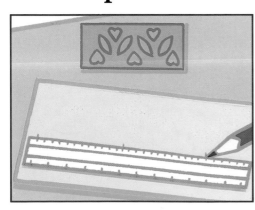

1. Cut out a simple pattern from cardboard about 6 in. long. Draw a straight line on the paper you want to stencil. Make a mark every 6 in. along the line.

2. Put the stencil card on the paper, with the bottom edge of the card running along the line, as shown. This will help keep the pattern straight.

3. Dab paint through the stencil and wait for it to dry. Move the card between the marks, and stencil. Repeat until you have finished.

BEAUTIFUL BUBBLES

Bubble painting is great fun and the patterns you get are always different. You can use bubbles to make pictures or decorate sheets of paper that you can make into many things. You will probably need to practice before you get a perfect bubble painting.

Things you need

Dish-washing liquid
Three or four cup-size
  containers
Lots of straws
Acrylic paints or India inks
Paintbrushes (for mixing)
Watercolor paper

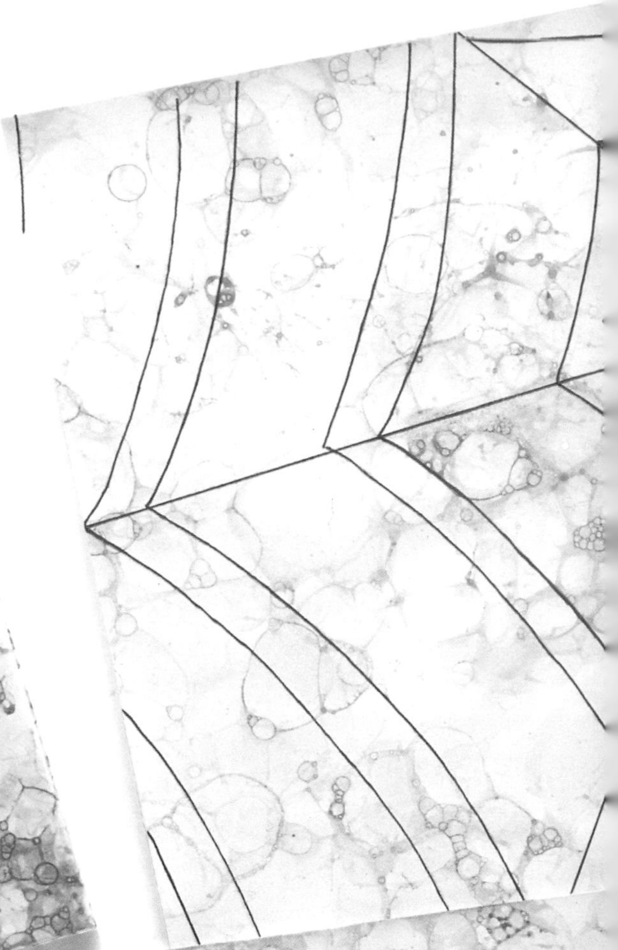

Spider in a spider's web

Bubbly book cover

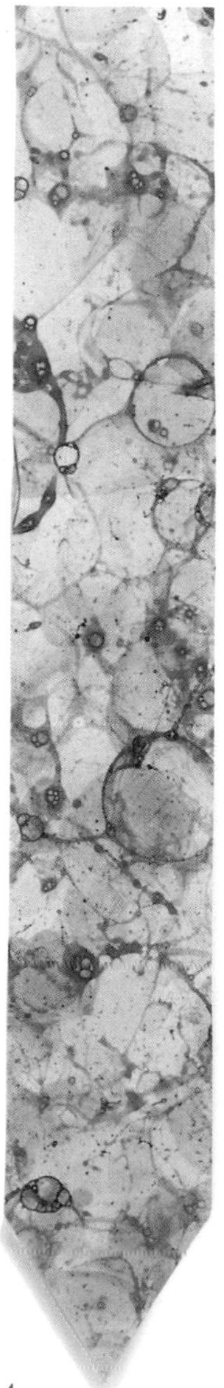

Bubbly bookmark

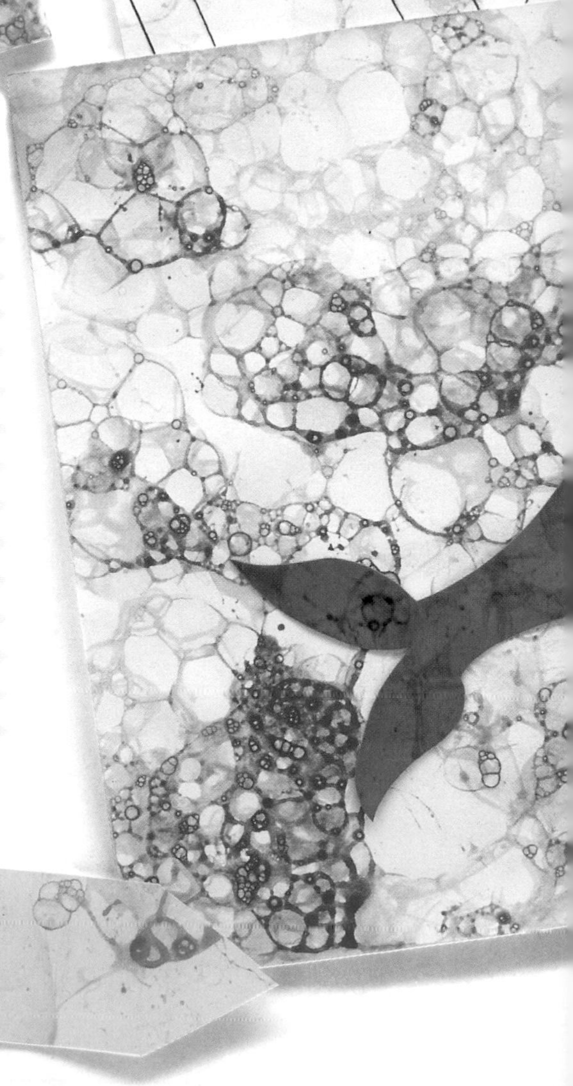

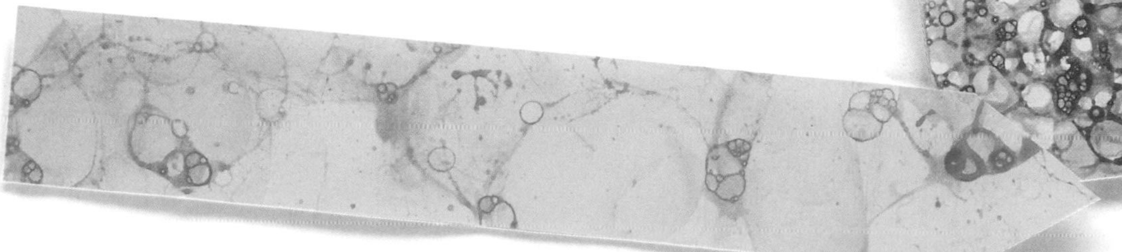

HANDY HINTS

Make sure you are close to a sink. You will need water for the bubble mixtures and for cleaning out containers when you change colors.

It's better to use thick paper because it dries flat.

You can use more than one color on a piece of paper. You don't have to wait for one color to dry before adding another. Bright acrylic paints show up the best.

Blowing bubbles

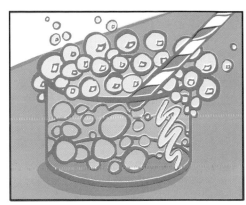

1. Squeeze about half an inch of dish-washing liquid into a plastic container. Add a spoonful of wet paint or ink and mix.

2. Add a few drops of water. Blow into the mixture with a straw until it bubbles over the edge of the container.

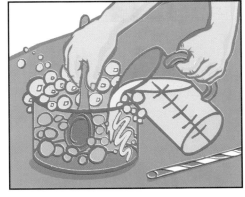

3. Put the paper over the container for a few seconds. When you lift it off you will see a pattern. Cover the paper with patterns.

4. If it doesn't work the first time, experiment with the bubble mixture. Add more water if it doesn't bubble properly.

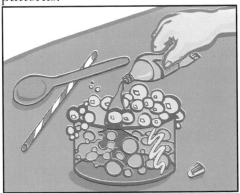

5. If the color is not strong enough to see, add more paint or ink to the bubble mixture, as shown.

6. Lay the finished bubble painting out flat on some newspaper to dry. Make another picture while you are waiting!

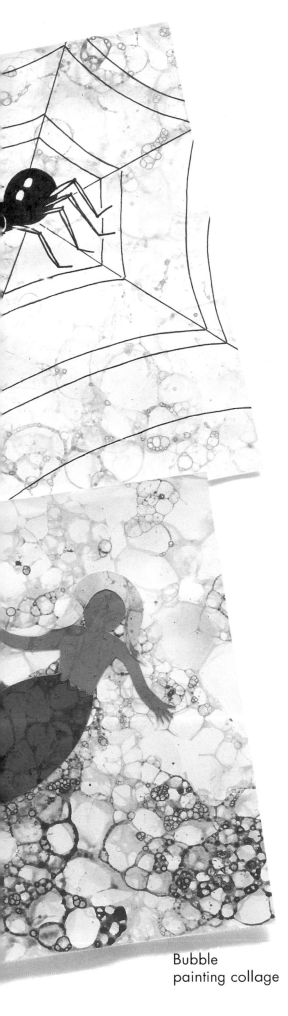

Bubble painting collage

75

MOBILE MAGIC

Here are some ideas on how to make bright and simple mobiles out of cardboard and paint. You may want to choose a theme when you design your mobile, such as this under-the-sea mobile, or this creepy-crawly one.

Things you need

Poster paints or acrylic paints
Thin cardboard, scissors, and
  pencil
Needle and colored thread
Big curtain ring

Under-the-sea
mobile to hang up
in the bathroom

Sea mobile

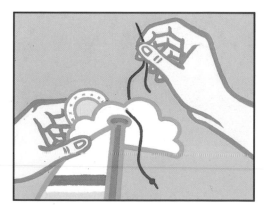

1. Draw a boat shape, as shown, on thin cardboard. Draw nine sea animals or plants.

2. Paint the shapes on one side using different-colored paint. Let the paint dry and cut out the shapes. Now paint the other sides.

3. Thread the needle and knot one end of the thread. Push the needle through the top of the boat and pull the thread until the knot stops it.

For a creepy-crawly mobile, cut out and paint a big sunflower shape. Hang three rows of creepy-crawly creatures from the flower.

HANDY HINTS

Instead of using thread, you can use pieces of yarn. For this you need a needle with a big eye.

You can also hang rows of mobile shapes from a wire or wooden coat hanger that you have painted.

Try different ways to decorate your mobile shapes, such as splattering, sponging, combing, or brushing.

To make a slithery snake mobile, draw a coiled-up snake on some thin cardboard. Cut it out and paint it with poster paints. Push thread through the snake's tail.

4. Thread the needle again and knot one end of the thread. Push the needle through the bottom center of the boat and pull the thread through, as shown.

5. Push the needle through the top of a sea shape. Cut the thread and tie it in a knot so it hangs down from the boat. Attach another sea shape.

6. Hang three rows of sea shapes from the boat, as shown. Tie a curtain ring to the thread at the top of the boat and hang it on a hook.

PREHISTORIC PAINTING

Prehistoric people were the very first artists. They drew on cave walls using colors made from things like charcoal or soil mixed with water. On these two pages there are ideas for making your own natural paints from things you can find outside, or in the kitchen.

Things you need

Thick paper
Brushes or twigs for painting

Colors you can make

Brown	-	tea/coffee and water
Brown	-	soil and water
Black	-	charcoal
Yellow	-	turmeric
Yellow	-	orange peel
Yellow	-	mustard powder and water
Orange	-	chili powder
Orange	-	carrot
Green	-	grass
Green	-	green pepper juice
Green	-	herbs
Blue	-	cornflower petals
Pink	-	sweet red pepper juice
Red	-	ketchup

Paint a jungle scene and outline it with charcoal.

Natural house and garden

1. For a green grass color, pick a handful of grass. Fold it in half and rub it on a sheet of white paper.

2. To paint the brown parts, mix some water with a little soil from the garden. Different types of soil will make different shades of brown.

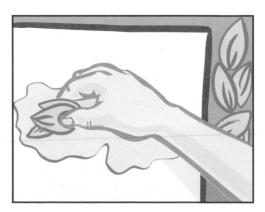

3. Collect some blue flower petals for a sky blue color. Wet them slightly and then rub them on the paper so that the color comes off.

HANDY HINTS

Mix tea leaves or coffee with water to get a pale brown-beige color, like old paper.

If you mix colored spice powders, such as paprika, with margarine, the mixture spreads easily and smoothly.

Don't try making paints from berries or fungi of any kind. Some of these are very poisonous. If you do use chili powder, wash your hands well and don't rub your eyes.

Natural house and garden

4. Rub fresh, slightly damp herb leaves, such as parsley or basil, on the paper to get shades of tree green. Your picture will smell of the herbs you use.

5. Mix ground kitchen spices, like chili powder, with soil and water to get yellow and orange colors. Your picture will smell spicy.

6. For another yellow, use a spice called turmeric mixed with water. For pink parts, squeeze the juice out of a red pepper.

PAINTED POTS AND PEBBLES

These colorful flowerpots and pebble paperweights are easy to paint and make good presents. You can decorate many other things with paint as well, such as paper plates, wooden spoons, sticks, driftwood, and shells.

Things you need

Acrylic paints, paintbrushes, and drawing paper
Plate and clear gloss varnish
Terra-cotta flowerpots
Big, flat pebbles

Paint a wooden spoon with one color and decorate to hang in the kitchen.

Pretty painted pot

1. Before you start, decide what to paint on your pot. Draw a design on paper and color it in. Put the flowerpot on an old plate.

2. If you want a background color, paint it on first and let it dry. Then paint your design on top. Use thin brushes for delicate lines and fat ones for bigger patterns.

3. Once the pot is dry, use a thick brush to cover it with a clear gloss varnish. If you want an extra-shiny pot, brush on another coat. Try painting a face or animal on another pot.

Use lots of colors when you paint your pots.

HANDY HINTS

Don't worry if you make a mistake while you are decorating your pots and pebbles. Wait until the paint is dry and then paint over the top.

Put your pot or pebble on a plate to paint it. You can turn the plate around as you paint so that you do not have to touch the wet pot.

Make strange creatures out of painted pebbles.

Paint and varnish paper plates for a wall decoration. But don't eat off them!

Pebble paperweights

1. Before you start, find flat, smooth pebbles or pebbles with interesting shapes. The best place to find pebbles is a stony beach or near a riverbank.

2. Decide what you want your paperweights to look like. You can paint on faces, patterns, and scenes, or make them look like a particular animal, such as a bird, lion, fish, or spooky insect.

3. Paint the pebble all over with a background color, using acrylic paint. Let it dry. Then paint on a face or body, as shown. When the paint is dry, brush on two coats of varnish.

MARBLING MADE EASY

Marbled paper has beautiful patterns, and every sheet looks different. It looks hard to do, but it's really very easy. You can use it as writing paper, for wrapping presents, for covering books, or to make a fabulous fan. Marbling can be messy so you should wear an apron and rubber gloves.

Things you need

Oil-based paints (If you use thick oil paints, you need to thin them with turpentine. Have a grownup help.)
Thick drawing paper and newspaper
Two or three paintbrushes
A shallow baking tray
Vinegar

Marvelous marbled writing set

Strips of marbled paper make good napkin rings.

Marbled gift tags

Marbling paper

1. Make sure that the piece of paper you are going to marble fits into the baking tray. Almost fill the tray with water. Mix in a splash of vinegar.

2. Use a paintbrush to dribble and splatter different-colored paint onto the water. If it's thin enough, the paint will float on top of the water.

3. Use up to four colors. Try swirling them around with a stick, blowing the paint around with a straw, or adding blobs with a brush.

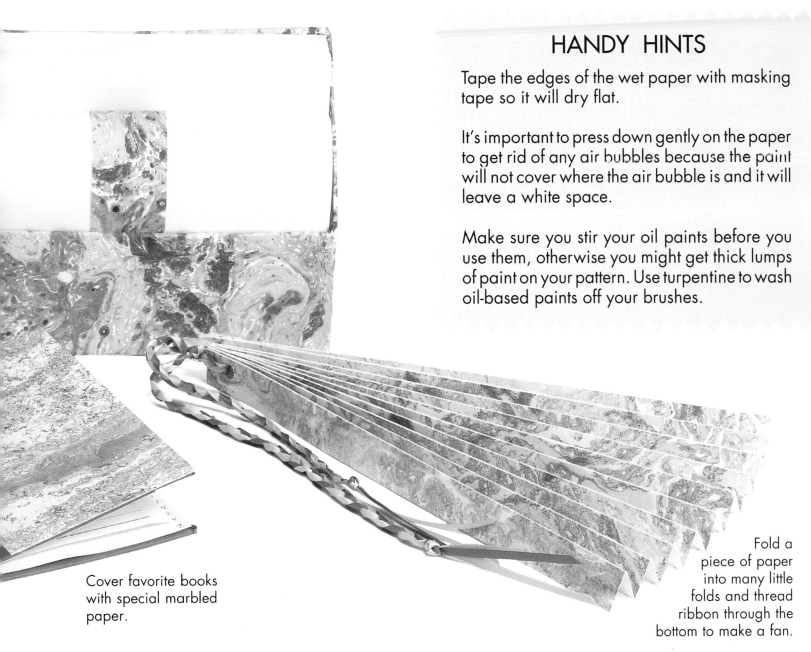

Tape the edges of the wet paper with masking tape so it will dry flat.

It's important to press down gently on the paper to get rid of any air bubbles because the paint will not cover where the air bubble is and it will leave a white space.

Make sure you stir your oil paints before you use them, otherwise you might get thick lumps of paint on your pattern. Use turpentine to wash oil-based paints off your brushes.

Cover favorite books with special marbled paper.

Fold a piece of paper into many little folds and thread ribbon through the bottom to make a fan.

4. Gently put the paper on the top of the water facedown. Tap it very softly with your finger, as shown, to get rid of air bubbles underneath.

5. After a few moments, lift the paper with both hands, holding opposite ends. Let the water drain off the paper into the tray below.

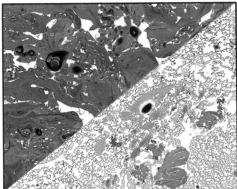

6. Put the paper on newspaper and let it dry. Before you throw the water away, try some more marbling. The pattern will be lighter each time.

WET PAPER PAINTING

You can get all sorts of interesting and exciting effects by painting on wet watercolor paper. It's very useful for making sky and landscape pictures. Try using poster paints, or use watercolors for a more watery look.

Things you need

Paintbrushes and poster paint
Watercolor paper
Container of water

HANDY HINTS

Try brushing lots of different-colored paints on wet paper. Hold the paper over a sink so that all the colors run together and the extra paint drips off. Turn the paper to make the colors run in different directions.

Farmhouse painted on a wash background.

Watery landscape

1. Wet a sheet of watercolor paper by painting all over it with water, as shown. It's best to use a big, fat paintbrush for this.

2. Still using the big brush, paint different colors for the land and sky. The colors will mix together as you paint.

3. When your wash painting is dry, use it as a background for painting plants, buildings, or people.

Using watercolors

Pale yellow, pink, and blue are good for painting a sunset sky on wet paper.

Use watercolors on wet paper to make a still life, like these plums on a plate.

1. Sketch the basic shapes of the picture you want to paint, using a very light pencil on dry watercolor paper.

2. Wet a piece of paper. Then use the watercolors to get different effects of light and shade, and dark shadows.

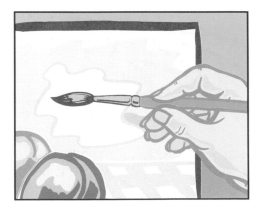

3. If you put one color next to another, they run together. Practice to see what kinds of pictures you can create.

85

SECRET PAINTINGS

The secret paintings on these two pages change when you want them to. The clever candle pictures are ideal for secret treasure maps, secret letters, and spy messages.

Things you need

White paper
Watercolor or poster paints
White candle
Pencil and paintbrush

HANDY HINTS

If you send a secret picture to a friend, don't forget to send instructions on how to make the picture appear.

It's a good idea to plan out your hidden painting before you start. You can sketch it first and paint over the lines.

This valentine heart is done with a red candle on red paper covered with white paint.

Grinning ghostly painting

Secret candle picture

1. Draw a picture or a secret message on white paper using the tip of a white candle.

2. When you want the picture to appear, paint over it with poster paint or watercolors.

3. The paint will not cover the waterproof wax and the white lines will show through.

Hidden
storm

Secret map
of hidden
treasure

Hidden storm painting

1. Draw and then paint a picture on a rectangular piece of paper. Let the paint dry.

2. Fold over about one-third of the paper. Complete the picture on the blank part, so that it joins the original picture.

3. Make some changes to the things you show on the folded part. When you open the flap, the picture will change.

87

PAINTING ON GLASS

If you paint a picture on a window it looks like stained glass when light shines through. Poster paints are best to use because they wipe off with water, but you can also use acrylic paints. You can also paint pictures and patterns on jars, glasses, and bottles.

Things you need

Poster or acrylic paints
Palette
Different-size paintbrushes
Ruler

Flowered glass

Birds in a tree bottle and glass

Blooming window box

1. Choose a window to paint on. Mix the colors you want to use and paint pots along the bottom of the window. Let them dry, then decorate them.

2. Paint flowers above the pots, either with a brush or by dabbing on wet paint with a scrunched-up tissue, as shown.

3. Paint on stalks and leaves. Paint in flower middles and other small details.

Noah's weather
window

Blooming
window box

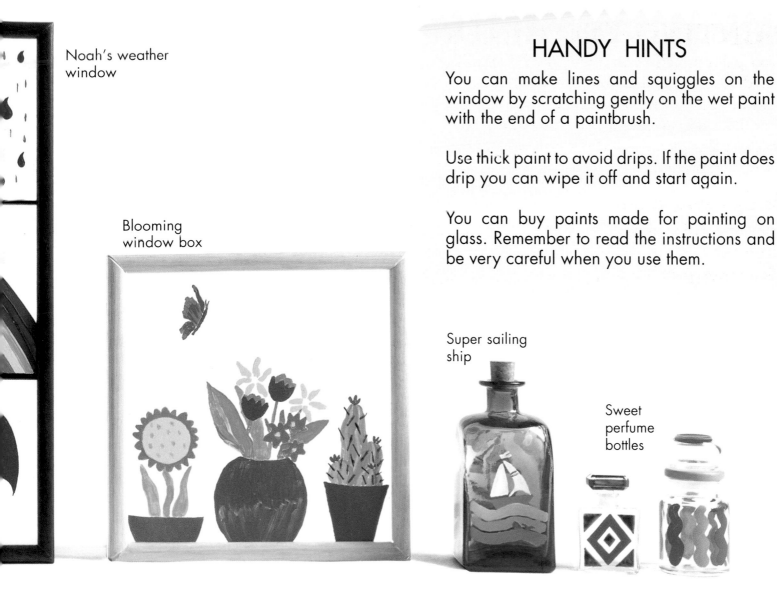

You can make lines and squiggles on the window by scratching gently on the wet paint with the end of a paintbrush.

Use thick paint to avoid drips. If the paint does drip you can wipe it off and start again.

You can buy paints made for painting on glass. Remember to read the instructions and be very careful when you use them.

Super sailing
ship

Sweet
perfume
bottles

Noah's weather window

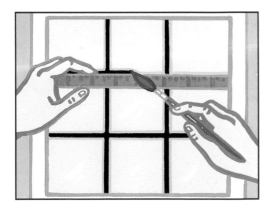

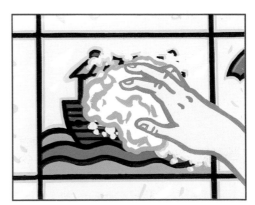

1. Paint nine squares in black paint to look like the black lead in a stained glass window. Run your brush along a ruler edge to get straight lines.

2. Paint a different picture inside each square. Shown here are an ark, weather symbols, an umbrella, and a snowman, but you can paint anything you want.

3. If you want to change the pictures in the future, do the black lines with acrylic paint. They will stay when you wipe off the poster paint pictures.

SILHOUETTE PAINTING

On a dark afternoon, paint a silhouette picture of a friend. Silhouette paintings are dark shadows or outlines painted on a much lighter background. You can also draw around figures cut out from old magazines and then paint in the figure shapes.

Things you need

Paper
Acrylic or thick poster paint
Paintbrushes and palette
Scissors
Cut out figures from old
　magazines or catalogs

Cut out and frame silhouettes of your friends.

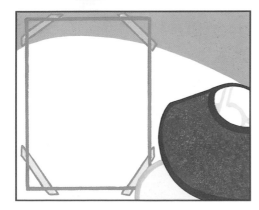

Face silhouette

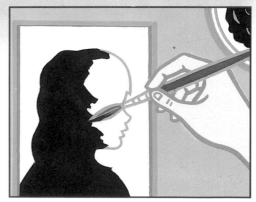

1. Close the curtains or wait until it is dark outside. Switch on a light. Then tape some paper onto the wall at about head height.

2. Ask a friend to stand sideways in front of the paper so that the side of his or her face casts a clear shadow on the paper. Your friend should not be too close.

3. Paint around the outline, or draw around it and paint the line afterwards. Take the paper down and paint in the head shape. Label the silhouette if you like.

90

If you are doing a face silhouette, try moving your friend closer or farther away from the paper. When he or she moves, the silhouette will change shape and size.

You can also paint a person's silhouette just by looking at them from the side, without using a shadow to help you.

You can cut out figures from a magazine, arrange them on some plain paper and paint around the edges with thick paint.

Figure silhouettes

Ask a friend to stand facing left and then right for this double silhouette.

Figure silhouettes

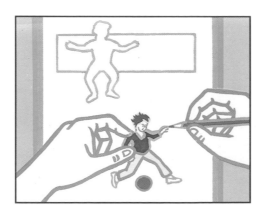

1. Cut out some figures from an old magazine or catalog. Arrange them on top of a sheet of white paper. Leave space around each figure.

2. Hold a figure down while you carefully draw around it with a sharp pencil so you have the outline of a figure. Do the same with the other cutouts.

3. When you have covered the paper with figures, paint inside the outlines. Try using other shapes cut out from old magazines.

ARTISTIC ICING

These two pages give you lots of ideas for painting on food, especially cakes and cookies, using white icing and food coloring. You can easily make your own icing or buy it ready-made at the supermarket.

Things you need

White icing (see recipe)
Rolling pin and cookie cutters
Food coloring
Thin paintbrushes and a wooden board
Plate or tray
Plain cookies or cupcakes

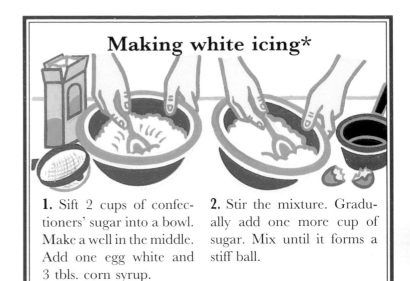

Making white icing*

1. Sift 2 cups of confectioners' sugar into a bowl. Make a well in the middle. Add one egg white and 3 tbls. corn syrup.

2. Stir the mixture. Gradually add one more cup of sugar. Mix until it forms a stiff ball.

Iced and painted cupcakes

Painted cupcakes

1. Use a rolling pin or your hands to press the icing out on a board. Cut circles to fit the cupcakes. Brush the cakes with jam or honey and stick on the icing.

2. Using food coloring, paint a different picture on each iced cake top. You can mix the food colorings together, or add water to make them paler.

3. Before you serve the cakes, put them on a plate or tray in the refrigerator for about 24 hours, or until the paint is completely dry on the icing.

*Ready-made icing may be used if salmonella poisoning is a concern.

HANDY HINTS

Wrap your icing in plastic wrap and put it in the refrigerator until you are ready to use it. The more you knead it, the softer it becomes.

To roll out icing, lightly butter a cutting board or dust it with confectioners' sugar. With clean hands, knead the icing to soften it. Use your palms to press it out to the thickness you want.

Icing animals

Christmas decorations

Icing cat

1. Roll some icing into two balls, one larger than the other. Make sure the icing is not too soft. Squash the bigger ball down onto a plate. This is the cat's body.

2. Press the smaller ball onto the cat's body, to make its head. Squeeze around the seam with your finger and a little water to stick the two firmly together.

3. Add some icing ears and a tail, as shown, and then paint the base color. Paint on a face and some whiskers. Put the cat in the refrigerator until it dries.

PHOTO PAINTINGS

Surprise your family and friends with these unusual photo paintings. They are easy to do and make good presents. All you need are photographs, cardboard, and poster paints. You can also make an advent calendar for Christmas using pictures cut out of magazines.

Things you need

Cardboard
Poster paints or watercolors
Strong glue, scissors, and tape
Photographs of your family, friends, or pets
Magazine pictures

Good luck card

Full house card

Full house card

1. Paint a picture of a house, with windows and a door. When the paint is dry, cut the windows and door on three sides to make flaps, as shown.

2. Tape photographs of your family or friends behind the flaps so that when you open the flaps from the front you can see all the faces.

3. Glue the picture to a big sheet of cardboard, as shown.

Fashion figures

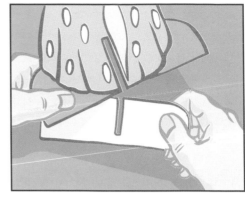

1. Cut the head off a photograph or off a picture of a person in a magazine. Stick the head on a piece of cardboard, as shown.

2. Paint clothes or a silly costume underneath the head. Cut out the whole figure, as well as a rectangular shape at the bottom, as shown.

3. Cut a slit in the middle of the rectangular piece of cardboard. Slide another piece into it to make a stand.

Fold up a strip of paper. Stick a different face onto each fold and decorate the backgrounds.

Fashion figures

HANDY HINTS

For an advent calendar, make 24 windows and a door. Cut out Christmas pictures from magazines to put behind them. Open one window each day until you reach the door on December 25.

SAND AND FLOUR ART

Poster paint mixed with sand or flour makes thick, bumpy paint. It is especially good for painting model scenes, such as landscapes or seascapes. You can also press leaves, twigs, or shells onto the paint before it dries to get an even more realistic scene.

Things you need

Poster paint and paintbrushes
Clean, dry sand
Flour
Cardboard
Plastic knife

HANDY HINTS

It's best to paint on thick paper or cardboard because thin paper is not heavy enough and becomes soggy and wet.

Cut a comb shape from stiff plastic packaging. Then drag it through the paint mixture to make different patterns.

Smiling sandy hippo

Sandy scene

Sandy scene

1. Mix poster paints with sand. Don't make the mixture too thick, or it will stick to your brush and won't spread easily over the paper.

2. Build a picture from the top of the page down. Start with the sky, then paint the middle of the paper, then the bottom.

3. Use a plastic knife to put the mixture on thickly. Try making waves and cuts in it. The tip of a brush is good for making lines and squiggles.

4. Press extra things, such as twigs, leaves, or tinfoil, onto the picture. For more texture, sprinkle sand on top of the wet mixture, as shown.

5. If you add flour and water to the sand mixture, it spreads thinner over a wider area. A mixture of flour and water makes good clouds or snow.

6. Let your picture dry overnight. When it is dry, you can rub some areas with your finger to make them smooth. Shake off any extra sand.

97

· CREATIVE CRAFTS ·

FUN WITH
FABRIC

· JULIET BAWDEN ·

MATERIALS, TIPS, AND HINTS

This section shows you how to make wonderfully original things using different types of fabric. It gives you ideas on how to decorate fabric with special fabric paints, felt-tip pens, glitter, and puff paints, as well as sequins, sparkles, buttons, and beads.

For many of the projects you can use scraps of fabric you can find around the house, but for some you may need to buy bigger pieces of fabric. The special techniques include simple appliqué, tie-dyeing, easy weaving, and printing on fabric with vegetables and spaghetti.

Things to collect and save

Scraps of plain or patterned fabric
Scraps of brightly colored felt
Old buttons
Colored ribbon and string
Sequins and beads
Stiff cardboard or posterboard
Embroidery thread in
  different colors
Small balls of yarn
Old baseball caps
  or berets
Old blue jeans

Making things can be messy. Before you start, put sheets of old newspaper on the floor. Remember to pick up pins, needles, and scissors when you have finished.

Wash your paintbrushes after you have used them, and store them in a pot with the bristles pointing upward.

A ruler is useful for measuring and drawing and cutting straight lines. Use tailor's chalk to mark lines on the fabric.

Useful tips

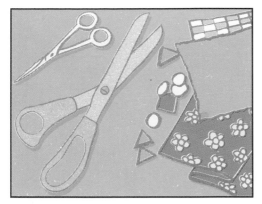

1. You will need a big pair of scissors for cutting big pieces of fabric, and a small pair for small delicate things. Be very careful when you are using them.

2. It is useful to have a pair of pinking shears. They are good for cutting out shapes from fabrics and trimming the ends of ribbons.

3. There are many kinds of special fabric paints and pens. You can find them in craft stores. Try experimenting with puff paints and glitter paints too.

4. If you are printing or dyeing fabric, wear an apron to keep your clothes clean. It is also a good idea to wear rubber gloves so your hands don't get stained with dye.

5. Remember to put tops and lids back on paints and glue to keep them from drying out. Wash any glue off your fingers so that you don't leave dirty finger marks.

6. If you want the things you make to look extra fancy, sew or glue on sequins, ribbons, sparkles, beads, and buttons. You can find these decorations in most department stores.

PAINTED PILLOWCASES

Have you ever thought of designing your own pillowcase for your bed? All you need is a solid-colored pillowcase and some fabric felt-tip pens. Cover it with stars or moons that will never wash out, like the one below, or design your own pattern. You can also try drawing a picture of yourself fast asleep on your duvet cover or sheet.

Look at your pajamas or nightgown to get an idea of how to paint a picture of yourself.

Things you need

Plain pillowcase,
  duvet cover, or sheet
Thin cardboard
Pencil or chalk
Scissors
Small sponge or toothbrush
Fabric felt-tip pens
  (including a black one)
Newspaper and masking tape

Try dabbing lots of different colors onto your pillowcase.

Seeing stars

1. Draw seven large star shapes and ten smaller ones on some thin cardboard. Carefully cut them out with small scissors. Put newspaper in the pillowcase to keep the paints from running.

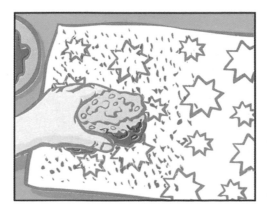

2. Arrange the stars on one side of the pillowcase. Then, with a small sponge or toothbrush, dab or splatter fabric paint around the shapes. Let the paint dry before you decorate the other side.

3. Use different colors on top of each other to get a really bright effect. Let the paints dry and then take out the newspaper. Turn the pillowcase inside out and iron it to set the color.

HANDY HINTS

To keep the pillowcase still while you are drawing on it, tape it across the corners to a table or the floor.

Your pictures will look much neater if you draw in one direction with the fabric felt-tip pens.

Instead of using fabric felt-tips, you can use fabric paint. The pens are easier to use, but the paint will go further. For big areas, dab on paint with a sponge.

Counting sheep pillowcase

A body in your bed

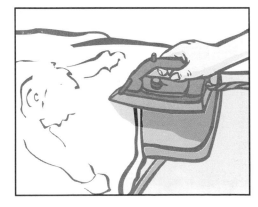

1. Put a white duvet cover on the floor and put flat sheets of newspaper inside it. Lie on top of the duvet with your arms stretched out. Ask a friend to draw around you with a soft pencil or chalk.

2. Stand up carefully. Make sure the shape is exactly how you want it to be. Then slowly go over the outline with a black fabric felt-tip pen. Add details, such as hair, a face, clothes, or pajamas.

3. Fill in the design with colored fabric felt-tip pens or fabric paints. Let it dry and then take out the newspaper. Turn the duvet cover inside out and iron it to set the color.

POTATO PRINT SHORTS

You may have already printed with cut-out potato shapes and paint on paper. Why not use the same idea to brighten up your boxer shorts or pants? Instead of using poster paint, you will need special fabric paint and some big potatoes or carrots to cut up into different patterns.

Things you need

Solid-colored shorts or pants
Fabric paint and a paintbrush
Felt-tip pen
Small vegetable knife
Newspaper and masking tape
Potatoes and carrots

Glue uncooked pieces of spaghetti onto a piece of thick cardboard. Brush paint over them and print lines over the potato prints.

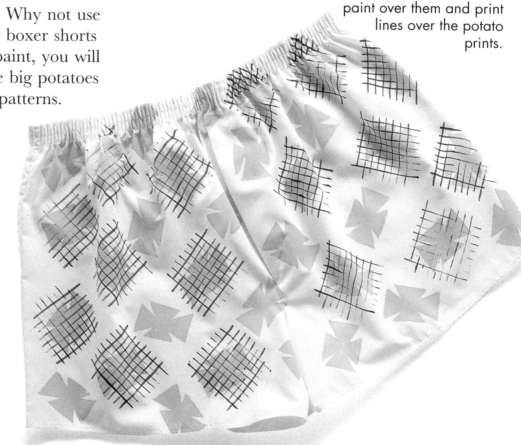

Use different-sized potatoes to make big and small shapes of the same design.

Printed boxer shorts make good presents.

104

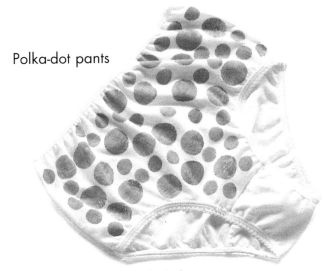

Polka-dot pants

Hearts and kisses

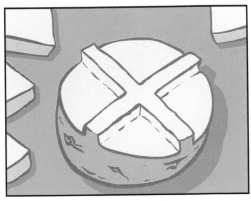

1. Carefully cut a big potato in half, widthways. Draw a big "X" on one half with a felt-tip pen. Cut around the **X** and cut away the rest of the potato so that the **X** stands out, as shown.

2. Stuff a pair of boxer shorts with newspaper to keep the paint from running through. Tape the shorts to a tabletop or the floor. Dab the cut potato with a tissue to mop up any extra potato juice.

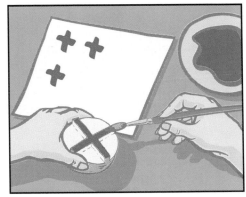

3. Brush paint onto the potato cut-out. Turn the potato over and print the pattern onto some paper to test it. If it looks good, print as many **X**s as you want onto the boxer shorts.

4. Now cut a different pattern out of the other half of the big potato, such as a diamond or heart shape, as shown. Brush a different color paint onto the heart and print this pattern on the shorts.

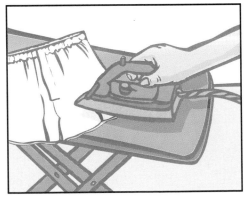

5. When the prints are dry, turn the shorts over and print on the back. Let the shorts dry. Then turn them inside out. Iron the shorts on the inside to set the color.

6. You can use carrots to print polka dots in lots of different colors. Cut off the top and brush paint onto the cut end. Use big carrots to print big dots, and little carrots for small dots.

COOL CAPS

These two pages show you how to make plain hats, caps, or berets look extra special. There are lots of ideas on how to decorate them with studs, puff paint, and fancy sparkles and sequins. You can also cover them with all sorts of bright felt shapes.

Fruit-salad beret

Flower-power hat

Things you need

Cap, felt beret, or straw hat
Sparkles and studs
Puff paints
Colored felt
Scissors
Fabric glue
Ribbon or ribbon rosebuds
Tracing-paper
Black felt-tip pen
Paper and pencil
Pins

Fruit-salad beret

1. To make this fruit-salad beret, first draw your design on paper. Draw any fruit you like, such as strawberries, oranges, grapes, and bananas.

2. Trace over the design and cut out each shape from the tracing-paper. Pin the tracing-paper shapes to the felt and cut them out.

3. Arrange the felt fruit shapes on the top of the beret. Pin them in place. One by one put glue on the back of each shape and glue it down.

Puff-paint cap

Use a simple design, such as squiggles and dots, when you decorate a cap with puff paint. To make the paint puff up faster, heat it with a hair dryer.

Sparkling studs

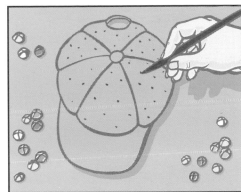

Before you start, mark the hat with a felt-tip pen to show where you want the studs to go. Push each stud from the front to the back of the cap, then close it.

Flower power

To make a pretty hat, cover a straw or felt hat with felt flowers, bows, or ribbon rosebuds. Glue or sew them around the brim of the hat.

Sparkling stud cap

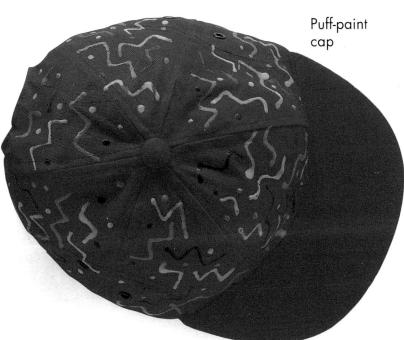

Puff-paint cap

HANDY HINTS

The prongs on studs are sometimes difficult to close. Try pushing each prong down with the blades of a pair of closed scissors.

When you are decorating a hat with felt shapes, arrange the shapes and pin them into position before you glue them down.

GLOW-IN-THE-DARK BANNERS

Make glow-in-the-dark banners to hang up in your bedroom. All you need is some black fabric and some special fluorescent fabric paints. You can decorate the banners with spooky monsters and ghosts, or design a super space scene. The paints will glow for up to twenty minutes in the dark. To make them glow again just turn on the light for a few seconds.

Things you need

Black paper and white and colored chalks
One yard of black fabric
Fluorescent fabric paints
Newspaper and masking tape
Fabric glue
Ribbon or string
Two thin dowels, each
    about 18 in. long

Glow-in-the-dark
night scene

Spage-age banner

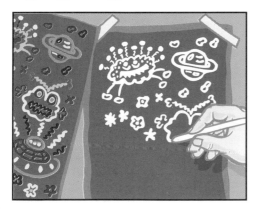

1. Before you begin, draw your design on black paper, using colored chalk. Tape the black fabric to a tabletop. Copy your design onto the fabric with white chalk, as shown.

2. Go over the outline of your design with fluorescent paints. Fill in any details. Squeeze the tubes very gently so that the paint comes out slowly. Let the paint dry.

3. If you want to make your banner extra fancy, add fake beady eyes, sequins, or sparkles. To stick eyes on, put blobs of paint on the fabric and press the eyes into the paint.

HANDY HINTS

Glow-in-the-dark fabric paint usually comes in a plastic tube with a nozzle. Do not press too hard, or the paint will come out too fast and your designs may smudge.

It is a good idea to have paper towels or rags handy to catch any drips while you are painting.

If you want to cover a large area with paint, spread it on with a piece of cardboard or a flat ice-cream stick.

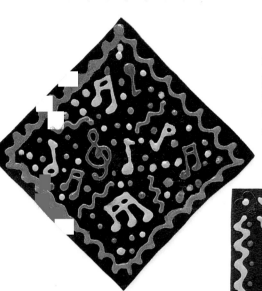

Make glow-in-the-dark badges to sew on your jacket or jeans.

Space-age banner

4. To make the banner, turn the sides of the fabric under by about ½ in. Stick them down with fabric glue. Lay the fabric face down and put one dowel near the top edge, as shown.

5. Roll the fabric around the dowel and glue it down firmly with fabric glue, as shown. Glue the second dowel to the bottom edge of the banner in the same way.

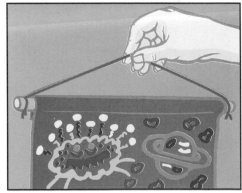

6. When the glue is dry, cut a piece of ribbon a little longer than the width of your banner. Tie the ends to the top dowel, as shown. Hang the banner up in your bedroom and watch it glow.

109

REALLY RAG DOLL

Here is a rag doll with a real difference. You can make it without any sewing at all. All you need are lots of colorful strips of fabric, string or yarn, and a ball for the doll's head. It makes a very good present to hang on the wall or just to decorate someone's bed.

Really rag girl doll

Things you need

White, red, and patterned fabric
Yarn, string, or thin ribbon
Small, soft ball
Scissors

Strips of fabric

Head/Body	7 white strips 1 in. x 27 in.
Arms	16 strips 1 in. x 8 in.
Skirt	19 strips 1 in. x 24 in.
Bodice	1 long red strip 1½ in. x 44 in.
Scarf	1 red square 9 in. x 9 in.

Rag girl

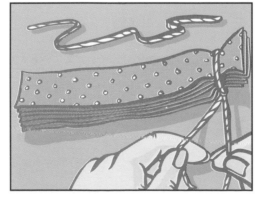

1. Cover the ball with the white strips of fabric, three across and four in the other direction. Twist the strips at the neck and tie them together with yarn.

2. Make a long bundle out of all the arm strips, as shown. Tie a piece of yarn about 1 in. from each end, to hold the strips of fabric together.

3. Divide the white neck strips in half. Put the arms between them. Tie yarn around the white strips, as shown, to hold in the arms at the waist.

Baby rag doll

Really rag boy doll

Rag boy

4. Tie another piece of string loosely around the waist. Loop the skirt strips over it, one at a time. When they are placed evenly around the doll, tighten the string.

5. For a scarf, fold the square in half and tie it around the doll's head. Wrap the bodice strip around the neck, cross it over at the front, and tie it at the back.

For a boy doll, divide the skirt strips in half. Leave one in the middle. Tie each half with yarn. Tuck the middle strip between the legs and loop it over the waist tie.

AMAZING ANGELS

On these two pages you can find out how to make angels out of scraps of cloth. They make wonderful decorations to hang on a Christmas tree, or just to hang on a wall. Instead of making an angel, you can leave the wings off to make a little cloth doll.

Things you need

½ yard of fabric
Yellow or patterned fabric
  for the dress
Paper and pencil
Scissors
Pins, needle, and thread
Red and black felt-tip pens
Polyester fill
Embroidery thread
Thin ribbon

Smiling angel

Make a big angel for the top of a Christmas tree.

Make different-colored angels.

Without the wings, the angels turn into little cloth dolls.

Smiling angel

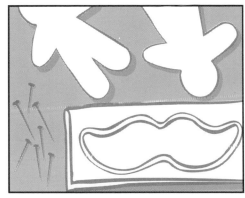

1. Draw a simple doll shape, about 6 in. high, on a piece of paper. Draw a wing shape, 7 in. long. Draw a ½ in. seam allowance all around the shapes. These are your patterns.

2. Cut out the patterns. Fold the fabric in half and pin the patterns to it. Cut them out so you have two fabric doll shapes and two fabric wing shapes. Take out the pins.

3. With the right sides facing, pin the doll shapes together and the wings shapes together. Sew around the edges. Leave a gap in the body and the wings as shown. Turn the fabric right side out.

4. Fill both the body and the wings with polyester fill. Sew up the gaps. Draw a T shape, as shown, on paper big enough to fit the angel's body. This is the dress pattern. Cut it out.

5. Fold the dress fabric in half and pin the pattern to it. Cut out two dress shapes. With the right sides facing, sew along the shoulders and down the sides. Turn the dress right side out.

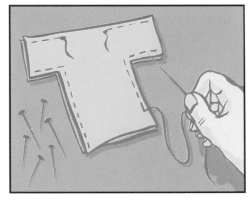

6. Slip the dress on the angel. Gather in the neck and neaten all the edges. Sew on the wings and a ribbon loop. Draw on a face. Make the hair by sewing on tiny knots of embroidery thread.

HANDY HINTS

When you are making the angel's body pattern, make the head connect to the body without a neck. This makes it easier to turn the angel right side out.

To make an angel that glitters, sew or glue sequins and sparkles onto the clothes.

If you don't have any polyester fill for stuffing, you can use tissues, cotton balls, or scraps of material instead.

Instead of making the hair out of embroidery thread, you can make long hair out of strands of yarn, and short hair out of furry material.

TERRIFIC TIE-DYE

Now you can make your own special tie-dye T-shirts covered with crazy, one-of-a-kind designs. All you need is a T-shirt, strong string, and fabric dyes. The great thing about tie-dye is that no two designs are ever the same!

Things you need

Light-colored T-shirt
Bucket and water
Cold-water fabric dye
Wooden spoon
Salt
Strong string
Vinegar
Apron and rubber gloves

Wacky tie-dye T-shirts

Tie-dye T-shirt

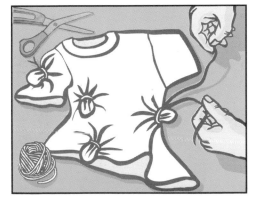

1. Wash and dry the T-shirt you are going to tie-dye. Clump together a little section of the shirt and tie it with strong string. Make a very tight knot. Make little clumps all over the shirt.

2. Put on the apron and rubber gloves. Follow the instructions on the packet of dye. Often the dye is first dissolved separately in warm water. Adding salt will create deeper colors.

3. Fill the bucket with water. Pour the dye mixture into the bucket. Stir the dye. Drop the T-shirt into the bucket of dye and push it down. Keep stirring it for about ten minutes.

HANDY HINTS

Always wear an apron, old clothes, and rubber gloves.

Hang the clothes in the bathtub to dry. Place garbage bags on the floor of the tub. When the clothes are dry, rinse tub and bags in cold water.

If you want to use more than one color, start with a light-colored dye and then use a darker one. Tie up new clumps and dip the shirt into the second color.

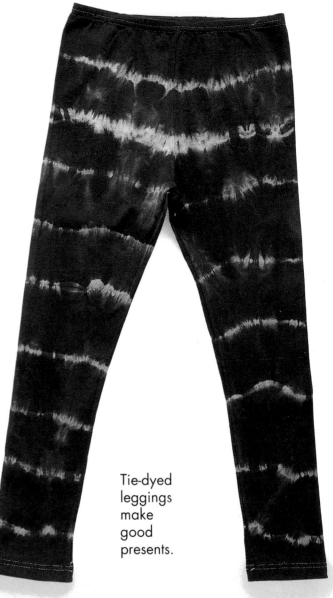

Tie-dyed leggings make good presents.

Tie-dye a long piece of fabric to make a swirly scarf.

4. Make sure that the T-shirt is completely covered with dye and leave it. Stir from time to time. After fifty minutes, take it out and rinse it under cold water until the water runs clear.

5. Hang the T-shirt up to dry. When it is dry, undo the clumps of fabric. Now you can see the cool patterns all over the T-shirt. The best results usually come from small, tight clumps.

6. Iron the shirt to take out the wrinkles the knots have made. To preserve the colors longer, wash the shirt with a little vinegar before you wear it.

115

RECYCLED RAGS

Do your favorite jeans have holes in them?
Instead of mending them with plain
patches, you can design your own fabric
pictures to patch them with. All you need
are scraps of fabric and some colorful
embroidery thread.

Things you need

Blue jeans, a skirt, or shorts
Scraps of fabric
Pins, needle, and strong thread
Embroidery thread
Scissors

Blanket stitch

1. Work from left to right with the thread at the top
edge of the fabric. Point the needle upward and push
it through the fabric from front to back, as shown.

2. Pull the thread out between the fabric and the
thread, as shown. Do this again and again until you
have sewn along all the edges of the fabric shape. Try
not to pull the thread too tight.

Make a patch
pocket and
sew it onto
your skirt.

Embroider
your initials
on your
blue jeans.

Before you sew on the patches, draw your design on paper.

HANDY HINTS

Try to find fabric decorated with pictures of animals or flowers. Cut them out and sew them onto your jeans.

If you don't like sewing, stick the shapes onto your jeans using an iron and fusible interfacing. This method is not as strong as sewing but it is very effective.

Pretty patches

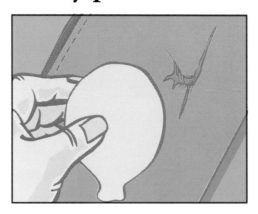

1. Measure the hole that needs patching. Then cut out a shape, like this big round balloon. Make it a little bigger than the hole so there is enough fabric to fold over for a neat hem.

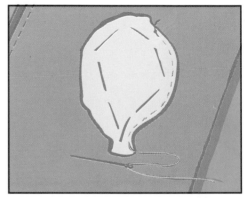

2. Pin the shape over the hole and sew it down with large basting stitches. Take out the pins. Then fold under the edges of the patch, and sew it down with small running stitches, as shown.

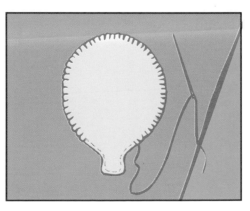

3. Decorate and neaten the edges with blanket stitch as shown in the box on the facing page. It is best to use doubled embroidery thread, as shown.

4. Add more shapes, such as a person or an animal. Sew them using stitches from steps two and three. Remove the basting stitches when you are done.

117

BEAUTIFUL BAGS

Instead of buying an expensive bag, why not make one for yourself? You can easily turn an old pair of blue jeans into a stunning shoulder bag decorated with felt, sequins, beads, or paints. Out of scraps of fabric, make a neck purse to carry money and other important things.

Things you need
for a blue jeans bag

Old blue jeans
Scissors and tape measure
Pins, needle, and strong thread
Ballpoint pen

for a neck purse

Piece of fabric, 5 in. long
 and 8 in. wide
Narrow ribbon, 30 in. long
Embroidery thread, ribbon, or lace
Needle and thread
Scissors and fabric glue
Fabric paints, buttons, sequins,
 and felt for decoration

Blue jeans bag

Cut out flower shapes from felt and sew or glue them all over the front of your bag.

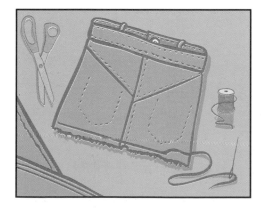

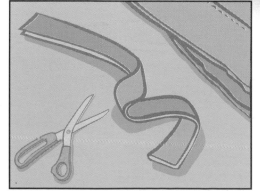

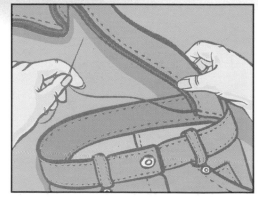

1. Turn the blue jeans inside out. Draw a line across them, where the legs meet the body. Cut along the line. Using a running stitch, sew along the bottom, as shown, to make a bag.

2. To make a shoulder strap for the bag, cut a strip of material, about 24 in. x 4 in., from one of the legs you have cut off. Then fold the strip of fabric in half along its length.

3. Fold over both the edges of the strap by ½ in. and pin them together. Sew along the edge. Then sew the two ends of the strap onto the inside of the blue jeans bag at the waist.

HANDY HINTS

Although you can glue some of the decorations to your bag, it is best to sew the seams, as they need to be strong.

If you are going to use fabric paints, draw the design on the material with a soft pencil before you start painting.

You can also make a bag out of an old pair of shorts. Sew on a bathrobe cord for the shoulder strap.

Nifty neck purses

Nifty neck purse

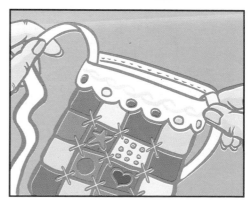

1. With the fabric inside out, turn in the top edge about ¼ in. and sew it down. Turn the fabric over and sew on a thin strip of lace. Decorate the fabric with buttons, puff paint, and felt.

2. Fold the fabric in half, with the decorated sides together. Then sew along the bottom and the open side, about ¼ in. from the edges, so that you have a small purse, as shown.

3. Stitch one end of the narrow ribbon to one side of the purse, close to the top. Stitch the other end to the other side of the purse. Then turn the purse right side out.

EASY WEAVING

These marvelous mats are woven out of yarn. They can be plain, striped, or patterned, and are fun and easy to make with a homemade cardboard loom. You can also weave small coasters for glasses and cups, a bookmark, and even a colorful purse.

Things you need

Cardboard (for the loom)
Ruler and pencil
Scissors
Darning needle
Small balls of yarn (cotton or wool)

HANDY HINTS

The threads that go up and down are called the warp. Join them in the center so the knots will be woven in.

The threads that go across are called the weft. Do not pull the weft too tight or the weaving will be uneven.

Make a set of colorful striped mats. Add pretty yarn fringes.

A cardboard loom

1. To make a loom, measure and cut a piece of stiff cardboard slightly larger than you want your mat to be. This loom is 7 in. long and 5 in. wide.

2. Draw two long lines across the cardboard, 1 in. from the top and 1 in. from the bottom. Mark short lines, ½ in. apart. Snip along the short lines to the long lines with small scissors.

3. To thread the loom, tie the end of some yarn to the top left-hand corner. Wind on the warp so that it goes up and down the front of the loom and under the slits, as shown.

How to weave

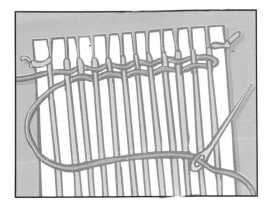

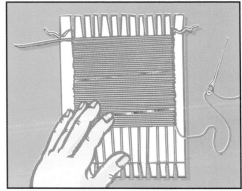

1. Thread the darning needle with yarn and start weaving under and over the threads of the warp. For the next row, weave over the threads you went under, and weave under the ones you went over.

2. Repeat these two rows until you have woven the length of the loom. As you weave, gently push each row close to the one above it to make sure the mat is nice and tight.

3. When you have reached the bottom of the loom, cut off the remaining yarn, and knot or glue down the end. Then carefully lift the mat off the loom so that you can use the loom again.

Weave some yarn into a big bright bookmark.

Striped mats

To make a purse, wind the warp thread onto the back and front of the loom. Weave first on the front of the loom and then on the back of the loom with the weft yarn doubled.

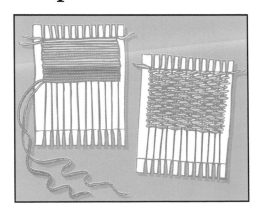

For horizontal stripes, weave five rows in one color and two in another. Weave the color you are not using into the side of the row you are working. To make vertical stripes, weave one row in one color, and the next in another color.

121

SACHET SWEETS

These sweet-smelling lavender bags look like candies. You can make them in different shapes and sizes, out of scraps of plain or patterned fabric. Fill a basket with sachets as a pretty table decoration or put them into drawers to make your clothes smell nice and fresh. If you can't find any lavender, try using dried rose petals or potpourri instead.

Things you need

Scraps of fabric
Dried lavender, rose petals, or
  potpourri
Thin ribbon and thread
Lace or embroidery anglaise
Scissors and pins
Fabric glue

Hang up a row of sweets glued or sewn to some ribbon.

Make big sweets to scent your clothes.

Fill a basket with sachet sweets made from scraps of felt.

To make glittery sweets, use shiny fabric decorated with sequins, sparkles, or glitter paint.

Sew a loop of cord on a sachet sweet and hang it over a coat hanger.

HANDY HINTS

It is much easier to make the sachet sweets if you do not fill them too full of lavender or potpourri.

Instead of using thread to tie up the ends of the sweets, you can use colorful rubber bands or yarn.

Sachet sweets

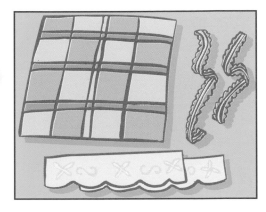

1. Cut out a piece of fabric, about 4 in. wide and 4 in. long. Cut two pieces of narrow ribbon and two strips of lace or embroidery anglaise, each about 4 in. long.

2. Spread glue along the inside of one of the ribbons and one of the strips of lace. Glue them to the right side of the fabric, along one edge, as shown. Do the same on the other edge.

3. When the glue is dry, glue a strip of fabric, about 1½ in. wide and 4 in. long, to the middle of the square piece of fabric, as shown. Instead of fabric you could use a piece of wide ribbon.

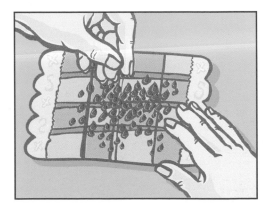

4. Turn the fabric square over and put a small pile of lavender or potpourri in the middle. Then fold in the top and bottom edges so that you have a little sausage shape.

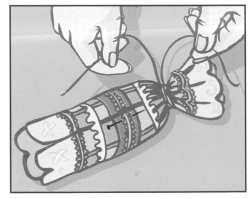

5. Hold the sausage shape together with a pin. Then cut a piece of strong thread and tie it tightly, about 1 in. from one end, as shown, so that it looks like a big candy.

6. Put more lavender in the open end of the sweet if it is not full enough. Tie up the end. Take out the pin and trim off the thread. Then tie a bow of thin ribbon over the thread at each end.

HANDY POT HOLDERS

Oven mitts and gloves make good presents, especially when they look bright and cheerful, like this funny face mitt and slithery snake glove. If you line them with thick batting, you can use them to hold hot pots, plates, and dishes. But be careful not to put them close to a flame or they will burn.

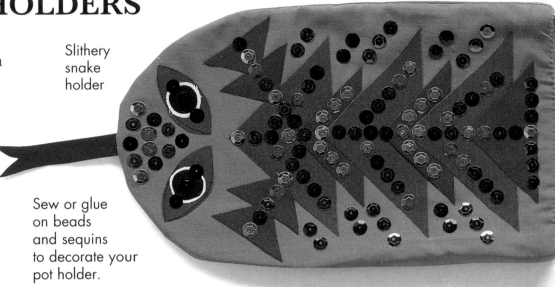

Slithery snake holder

Sew or glue on beads and sequins to decorate your pot holder.

Things you need

Pencil and paper
1 yard of plain fabric
½ yard of thick batting
Scraps of felt
Beads and buttons
Pins, needle, and thread
Scissors
Fabric glue
Ribbon

HANDY HINTS

It is easier to make an oven mitt without a thumb, but it is easier to hold hot things with a mitt that has one.

Make the gap in between the hand and the thumb extra big. Use a pencil to push the thumb the right side out.

To make an oven mitt that is big enough for an adult to wear, draw the pattern around an adult's hand.

Funny face

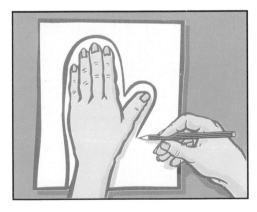

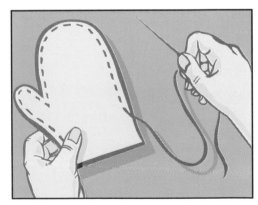

1. Draw around your hand on a sheet of paper, keeping your fingers together. Make the thumb extra big. Cut out the pattern, making it a little bigger than your hand all the way around.

2. Pin the paper pattern to the plain fabric. Cut out four gloves, as shown. Then pin the pattern to the thick batting and cut out two more gloves exactly the same size, as shown.

3. Pin two fabric gloves together with the right sides facing each other. Sew around three sides of the glove, as shown, ¼ in. from the edge. Turn the glove right side out.

Funny
face pot
holder

Try making a
patchwork pot
holder out of lots
of scraps of fabric.

4. Sew a batting glove onto each of the two remaining fabric gloves, as shown. Then, with the fabric gloves facing each other, sew another glove as you did the first one.

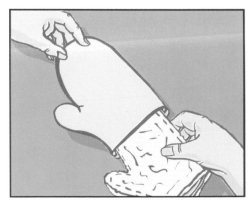

5. Keeping the glove inside out, slip it inside the first glove to make a thick lining. Fold in the edges of the inner and outer gloves at the wrist and sew them neatly together.

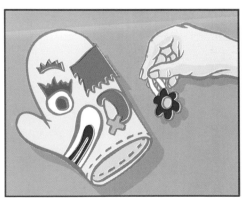

6. To make a funny face, cut out a felt mouth, eye, and ear and some felt hair. Glue them to the glove. Sew a loop of ribbon with a felt flower onto the bottom so you can hang up the pot holder.

125

FUNNY FINGER PUPPETS

Turn a pair of gloves into a pirate, a scarecrow, a soldier, a crazy clown, and a happy man. Or design your own finger puppets with animal or spooky fingertips. Make them for yourself or as a present for a friend. Small children will love wearing them.

Things you need

Solid-colored knitted gloves
Scraps of felt and fabric
Yarn, beads, buttons, and ribbon
Scissors, needle, and thread
Fabric glue and tissue paper

Amazing animal puppet

Funny finger people puppet

Finger people

1. For a pirate little finger, cut out a round felt head and a red nose. Cut out a beard, an eye and an eye-patch. Glue the features to the face and glue the face onto the glove.

2. Cut out two felt hats. Glue one to the front of the finger and the other to the back so they cover the top of the head. Decorate the hat and tie a fabric scarf around the neck.

3. Make a scarecrow for the next finger. Cut out felt eyes, a nose, a mouth, and two hats. Glue yarn hair to the head before you glue on the hats. Tie on a scarf.

4. For the soldier on the middle finger, cut out a face, mustache, a nose, and a hat with a chin strap. Sew on four tiny beads to finish off his outfit.

5. Make the clown on the fourth finger with cross-shaped eyes, a nose, a mouth, and a bright peaked hat with a flower. Gather ribbon for his collar and sew buttons below it.

6. The smiling man on the thumb has a shirt and collar, a bowtie, and a felt jacket. Cut out a face, and glue little eyes, a smiling mouth, and fuzzy yarn hair to it.

Make some spooky gloves to wear at Halloween.

HANDY HINTS

To keep the glue from sticking the fingers of the glove together, stuff each one with tissue paper before you start.

Make sure you do not sew the fingers together when you sew on the buttons or other decorations.

Glue the nose, eyes, and mouth to the face before you glue the face to the finger of the glove.

FANCY FEET

With special fabric paints and felt-tip pens you can make your sneakers look almost brand-new, even if they are quite old. If you want them to look extra cool, you can decorate them with strips of shiny sequins. Try painting pictures and patterns on your socks as well, or decorate them with buttons, beads, and tiny bells.

Things you need

Solid-colored sneakers
Solid-colored socks
Fabric paints and pens
Glitter and puff paints
Fabric felt-tip pens
Thin ribbon and
  ribbon bows
Buttons, beads, and bells
Paper and pencil
Newspaper and scissors

For super cool sneakers, use bright metallic ribbon for the shoelaces.

Paint swirls of shiny puff paint on sneakers.

Snazzy sneakers

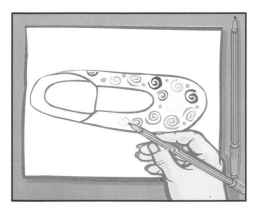

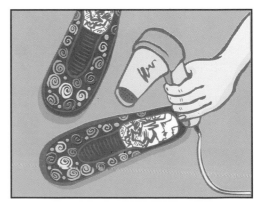

1. Before you start, decide what pattern you are going to paint on your sneakers. It is easier to paint a simple pattern, such as dots, stripes, or squiggles. Draw your design on a sheet of paper.

2. Stuff the sneakers with old newspaper and start painting on the design. Paint one shoe before you start the other, working from the front to the back, as shown. Use lots of different colors.

3. Squeeze little dots of puff paint in between the shiny swirls. Then let the paint dry. Use a hair dryer if you want the paint to dry faster. Then take the newspaper out of the sneakers.

Party socks

Painted socks

Jingling socks

Super socks

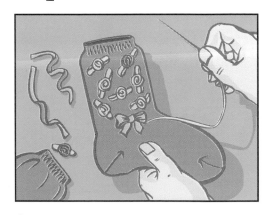

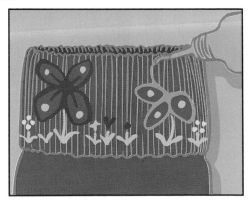

1. For pretty party socks, sew tiny ribbon roses around the top of plain socks. You can also make tiny bows out of thin, colorful ribbon and sew them onto the top of the socks, as shown.

2. Sew colorful beads around the top of a sock. These should only go as far as the ankle so they do not touch your shoes. If you would like noisy socks, sew on some tiny bells.

3. You can paint patterns on socks, using fabric paints, puff paints, and felt-tip pens. These do not wash off. If you want to make socks sparkle, use special fabric glitter paint as well.

PRETTY POM-POMS

These pretty pom-poms are simple and fun to make and can be any size you like. You can make them from all kinds of yarn and use them to decorate hats, belts, headbands, and gloves. You can also make funny pom-pom people, fluffy animals, and creepy-crawly caterpillars or snakes.

Things you need

Thin cardboard
Pencil
Scissors
Cup or small plate
Small balls of yarn

Cover a headband with sparkly pom-poms.

HANDY HINTS

It is best to use thin yarn for small pom-poms and thicker yarn for bigger, fluffy ones. The tighter you wind the yarn around the cardboard circle, the fluffier your pom-pom will be. Try experimenting with different kinds of yarn, such as mohair, yarn with sparkles, or even speckled yarn.

Sew different kinds of pom-poms together to make a creepy caterpillar.

Pretty pom-pom

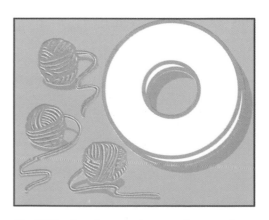

1. Draw two circles on thin cardboard by drawing around a cup or small plate with a pencil. Draw a smaller circle in the middle of each big circle, as shown.

2. Using small scissors, cut out the two big circles of cardboard. Cut out the two small circles in the middle. Put one cardboard ring on top of the other.

3. Wind a long piece of yarn into a ball, small enough to go through the hole in the middle of the rings. Make two or three small balls of yarn, as shown.

Make extra big pom-poms for a woolly hat.

Brighten up your gloves with pretty pom-poms.

Make a chirpy yellow pom-pom chick.

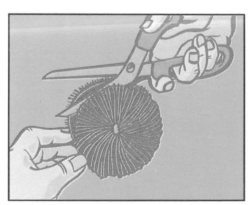

Mixed-up pom-poms

Striped pom-pom
To make striped pom-poms, wind thin layers of different-colored yarn around the cardboard rings, one on top of the other. Use four colors.

Polka-dot pom-pom
For polka-dot pom-poms, wind one layer of your main color yarn around the cardboard rings. Add thin strips, as shown, of another color on every other layer of yarn.

Squared-up pom-pom
For squared pom-poms, divide the rings into four quarters with a pencil. Cover each one with a different-colored yarn.

Sparkly pom-pom
To make a pom-pom that sparkles, you need to buy special yarn that looks as if it is full of tiny pieces of glitter.

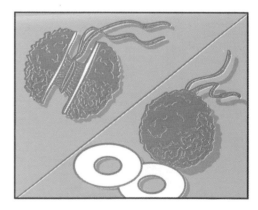

4. Wind the yarn around the two rings, as shown. Keep on winding until the rings are completely covered and only a tiny hole is left in the middle.

5. Then push one blade of the scissors between the two rings, as shown. Cut through all the yarn around the edges. Be careful not to cut the cardboard.

6. Pull the rings slightly apart and wind a long piece of yarn tightly around the middle of the pom-pom. Tie a tight knot. Then carefully pull off the rings.

131

T-SHIRT ART

With a little imagination you can transform a plain white T-shirt into something much more original and fun to wear. Draw on your own design and decorate it with bright fabric paints, special puff paints, sparkling glitter paints, or fabric felt-tip pens.

Things you need

White or solid-
  colored T-shirt
Paper and pencil
Newspaper
Masking tape
Fabric paints, puff
  paints, glitter paints,
  or fabric felt-tip pens
Tailor's chalk or very
  soft pencil
Embroidery transfers
Carbon paper
Iron

Cover a T-shirt with footsteps, using cut-out stencils.

Embroidery transfer T-shirt

Carbon-copy T-shirt

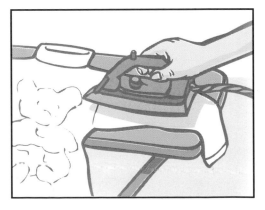

1. Before you start, draw your design on a big sheet of paper. Put a piece of carbon paper, ink side down, onto the front of a T-shirt. Put your design on top and trace over the design.

2. Take off the carbon paper. The design will show up on the shirt. Put sheets of newspaper inside the shirt and color in your design with glitter paint, puff paint, or fabric felt-tip pens.

3. When the paint has dried, take out the newspaper and turn the T-shirt inside out. Iron over the design on the wrong side to set the paint, so it can't be washed out.

132

As a birthday present, give a friend a T-shirt with his or her age on the front.

Carbon-copy T-shirt

Transfer T-shirt

1. Choose and buy the embroidery transfers you want to use for your design. Cut them out. Then tape them, one at a time, to the front of the T-shirt, as shown. Make sure you put them ink side down.

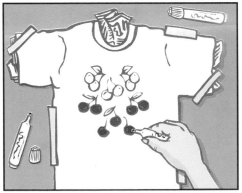

2. Carefully iron over the transfers, using a hot iron. Then remove the paper. The designs will now be on your T-shirt. Color them in with fabric paint, puff paint, glitter paint, or fabric felt-tip pens.

Permanent pictures

Make a picture on your T-shirt using different techniques, such as drawing, transfers, and stencils. Use different pens and paints. Let them dry before setting them with a hot iron.

QUICK-STICK PENCIL CASE

Make your own pencil case or toiletry bag quickly and easily without any sewing at all. All you need is some vinyl, sticky-backed felt, and some Velcro to keep it closed. You can also design a bigger bag for your swimsuit and towel.

Quick-stick
pencil case

Things you need

Sticky-backed felt
Sticky-backed Velcro, 9 in. long
Fabric glue and ruler
Ballpoint pen or pencil
Vinyl (available at fabric stores)

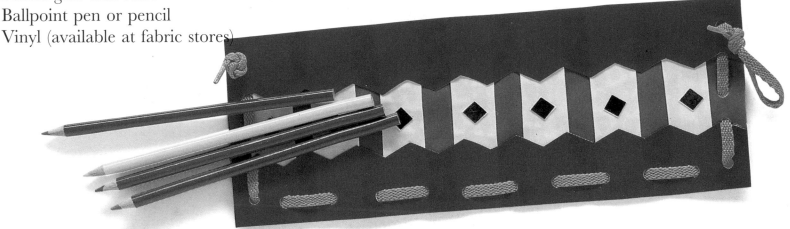

Make your pencil case longer
if you want to fit in a ruler.

Perfect pencil case

1. Draw two rectangles, each about 9 in. long and 4 in. wide, on the inside of the vinyl. Draw a ½ in. margin around both rectangles, as shown. Cut out the bigger rectangles.

2. Peel the backing paper off a strip of Velcro, 8 in. long. Stick it onto one of the long sides of one of the vinyl. Stick Velcro onto one of the long sides of the second rectangle.

3. To decorate the pencil case, cut out different shapes, such as these crayons, from sticky-backed felt. Stick them onto the back and the front of the outside of the rectangles.

134

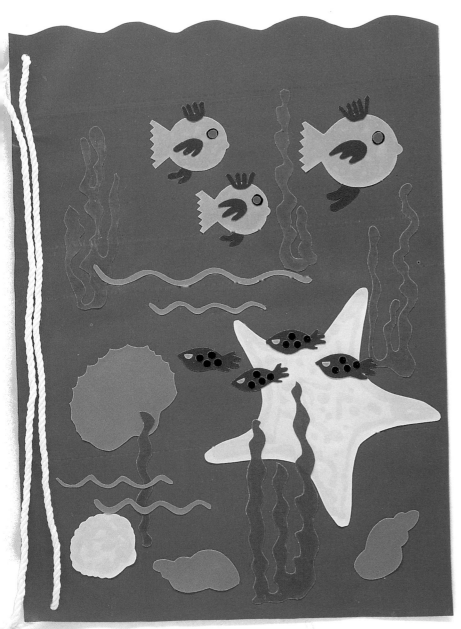

Decorate a beach bag with fish and other sea creatures.

Stick your name onto your toiletry bag.

Laced-up case

Toiletry bag

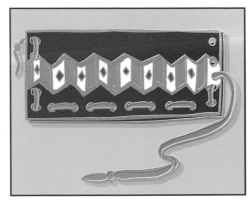

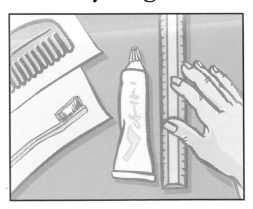

4. Spread glue around the three edges of one of the rectangles, inside out, as shown. Line up the Velcro so they match perfectly. Then stick the two rectangles together to make a pencil case.

As well as gluing the pencil case, you can tie it together with a shoelace to make it even stronger. Use a hole punch around three of the edges and thread the shoelace through the holes, as shown.

Make a toiletry bag in the same way as your pencil case. To work out the size, measure the things you are going to put inside, such as a toothbrush, comb, toothpaste, and shampoo.

JOLLY JUGGLERS

All you need to make these jolly juggling balls are small pieces of felt and dried peas, lentils, or rice. Try making a tossed-salad juggling set with a tomato, a cucumber, and green lettuce. Or give a friend a set of jolly juggler dice.

Things you need

Pencil, paper, and ruler
Scissors and pinking shears
Felt
Pins, needle, and thread
Dried peas, beans, rice, or lentils
Embroidery thread (for decoration)

Make three jolly juggler dice out of black, red, and white felt.

Make jolly jugglers with names.

Tossed-salad set

HANDY HINTS

Make a small paper funnel to use when you are filling your juggling balls. Do not overfill the balls or they may burst open at the seams.

If you do not have any felt, use any scraps of fabric you can find. Sew the fabric with the inside out, to keep it from fraying. Then turn it right side out.

Jolly
jugglers

Jolly jugglers

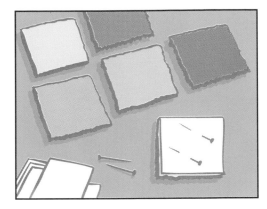

1. Draw six squares, each 2 in. by 2 in., on paper. Cut out the squares and pin each one to a separate piece of felt. Cut out the felt squares and take out the pins.

2. Sew three different-colored squares of felt together, as close to the edges as possible. Now you have a row of squares, as shown. Do the same with the other three felt squares.

3. Sew the two rows of felt squares together so they form a cube shape, as shown. Leave one side open and fill the cube with dried peas, beans, or rice. Then very neatly sew up the last side.

Tossed-salad balls

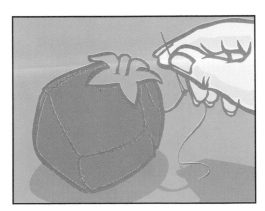

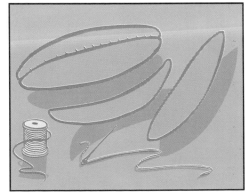

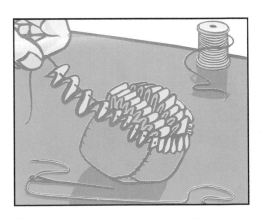

1. To make a tomato juggling ball, make one jolly juggler (see above) using red felt. Cut out a small green star shape and sew it to the top of the juggler as a stem, as shown.

2. For a cucumber, cut two green crescents and two ovals, about 6 in. long and 1½ in. at the widest point. Sew them together, alternating the ovals and crescents.

3. To make a lettuce juggling ball, make a jolly juggler 3 in. by 3 in. using green felt. Cut out extra strips of felt with pinking shears. Gather the strips and sew them onto the juggler, as shown.

AWESOME APRONS

Aprons make good presents as well as being very useful. These two pages show you how to make your own apron and some ways you can decorate it. You can create a special cook's apron with cooking tools, an artist's apron, or a flowery apron for a gardener.

Things you need

½ yard thick cotton fabric
1½ in. x 20 in. bias tape
  or strong, wide ribbon
Pins, needle, and thread
Soft pencil
Fabric pens and paint
Newspaper and masking tape
Fabric glue

Look in the kitchen to get an idea of the tools to paint on your clever cook's apron.

Messy artist's apron

Clever cook's apron

1. To make the paper pattern, draw a rectangle, 16 in. wide by 2 ft. long, on newspaper. Cut it out. Draw two lines, each about 4 in. long, 7 in. from the top of the rectangle.

2. Draw two lines from the two 4 in. lines, straight up to the top of the paper. On one side draw a big curve, as shown. Fold the paper in half lengthwise and cut out the curve.

3. Open the apron pattern. Pin it on the fabric and cut it out. For the pocket, cut a piece of fabric 11 in. wide and 7 in. deep. Turn under and pin the edges. Sew or glue them down.

HANDY HINTS

The measurements for the aprons are just a guide. You may want to make your apron bigger or smaller, longer or wider.

Hold a flat sheet of newspaper against you or the person you are making the apron for. Ask someone to help you measure the size you need.

Use fabric paints and puff paints to draw flowers on the busy gardener's apron.

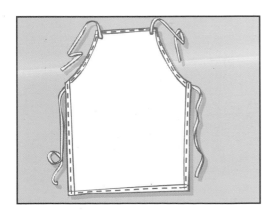

4. Turn under and pin the edges of the apron. Sew or glue them down. Then sew the four cotton tapes in place, at the top and sides of the apron, as shown.

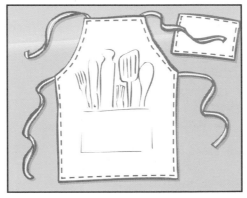

5. Pin the pocket in place and mark it with a pencil. Take it off. Tape the apron to a table and draw some cook's tools with a soft pencil. Make them look as if they are standing in the pocket.

6. Color in the cook's tools with fabric pens and paint. Iron the back of the apron to set the colors. Pin the pocket to the apron and sew it in place, using a neat running stitch.

COZY CHRISTMAS STOCKINGS

On these two pages, you can find out how to make cozy Christmas stockings for the whole family. It is best to use felt as it does not fray and is easy to decorate with sequins, beads, and bits of fabric. As well as making big stockings, try making a string of little ones to hang across the fireplace or in a window.

Things you need

Paper and pencil
Scissors
Large pieces of felt
Large boot or sock
Pins, needle, and thread
Pinking shears
Beads, sequins, buttons,
  scraps of felt, ribbon,
  and sparkles for
  decoration
Thin ribbon
Fabric glue

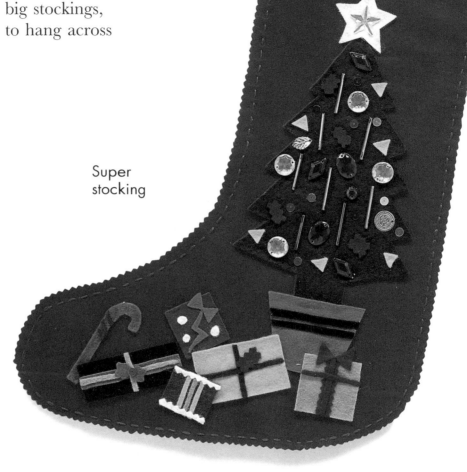

Super
stocking

Super stocking

1. Put a big sock or a boot on paper. Draw around it. Take the sock off the paper and cut out the sock pattern, making it a bit bigger all the way around.

2. Pin the paper pattern to a big piece of felt and cut it out with pinking shears. Repeat so that you have two felt sock shapes. These will be your stocking.

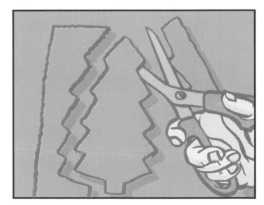

3. Draw a big Christmas tree shape on paper. Cut it out, pin the pattern to felt that is a different color than the stocking, and cut out the felt tree. Take out the pins.

140

Glue different felt pictures on each of your tiny stockings.

HANDY HINTS

Make sure all the decorations you have glued to the stocking are dry before you sew the front to the back. It is best to sew on things like buttons and bows.

You can use another fabric for the stocking, but choose one that does not fray. Cut the edges with pinking shears.

4. Using paper patterns, cut a big pot shape out of felt for the tree to stand in. Then cut present shapes out of different-colored felt, as shown.

5. Spread glue on the back of the tree shape and stick it onto one of the stockings. Glue the pot underneath the tree, and the presents around the pot.

6. Decorate the tree with sequins, sparkles, and felt shapes. Sew the two sides of the stocking together with embroidery thread. Sew a loop of ribbon on the top.

141

MERRY CHRISTMAS DECORATIONS

These Christmas decorations will make your tree look bright and cheerful and will last for a long time. You can make felt decorations in different shapes, and decorate them with beads, sequins, buttons, and ribbon. Hang the decorations on a tree or give them away as presents.

Decorate the front and back of the decorations.

Things you need

Felt
Batting and thin ribbon
Sparkles, beads, glitter glue, and sequins
Scissors or pinking shears
Pins, needle, and thread
Paper and pencil
Fabric glue

Use gold or silver thread to sew your decorations together.

Sparkling tree

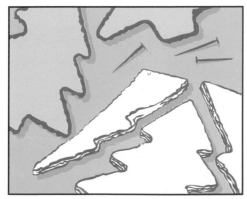

1. Draw a Christmas tree, about 5 in. tall, on paper. Cut it out and pin it to a piece of felt, folded in half. Cut out two felt trees. Cut the same tree shape from a piece of batting.

2. Make a sandwich of the two felt trees with the batting in the middle. Pin them all together and then sew them together, as close to the edges as possible, as shown. Sew on a felt pot.

3. Take out the pins and decorate the tree as if it were a real tree. Sew or glue on beads, sparkles, and strips of sequins. Sew a loop of ribbon on the top of the tree so you can hang it up.

Glitter stocking

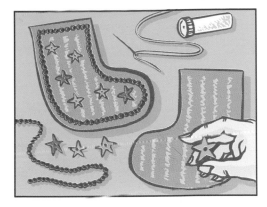

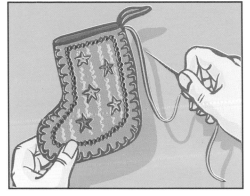

Hearts and stars

1. Using a paper pattern, cut two Christmas stocking shapes out of felt. Sew or glue a few sequins onto the stockings, leaving the edges free. Decorate the stockings with glitter glue.

2. Sew the two stocking shapes together, as close to the edge as possible. Leave the top open so that you can fill the stocking with tiny presents. Sew a loop of ribbon to the top of the stocking.

Make lots of heart, moon, and star decorations, following the same directions as for the sparkling Christmas tree. Decorate them with strips of sequins, glitter glue, and sparkles.

Sequin stars, hearts, and moons

HANDY HINTS

To give the decorations pretty edges, cut out the felt shapes with a pair of pinking shears.

Some of these decorations are stuffed with batting to make them nice and thick. Or you can stick two pieces of felt together instead.

If you are not very good at sewing, cover the stitches with beads, braid, or a strip of sequins.

You can buy sequins in many different shapes and sizes.

· CREATIVE CRAFTS ·

MAKING
PRESENTS

· JULIET BAWDEN ·

MATERIALS, TIPS, AND HINTS

In this section there are all sorts of easy but exciting presents for you to make. There are presents for babies, brothers and sisters, friends, moms, dads, and grandparents.

You can probably find most of the things you need to make them with around the house, but you may need to buy a few special things.

Before you start making a present, read the instructions carefully to find out what you need. The Handy Hints give you lots of extra ideas and help you make the presents.

Things to collect

Cardboard boxes and plastic containers (like those for yogurt or margarine)

Cardboard tubes (like those for paper towels) and egg cartons

Cardboard — such as empty cereal boxes and the backs of notepads

Paper — old newspapers, scraps of colored paper, used stamps, drawing paper, old magazines, old wrapping paper, birthday cards, and old postcards

Used lollipop sticks, ice cream sticks, garden markers, or thin straight sticks

String, ribbon, wool, corks, tinfoil, toothpaste or tomato paste tubes, Plasticine, bag ties, paper clips, buttons, and beads

Useful tips

1. You will need poster paints or tempera paints for some of the presents you make. Ready-mixed poster paints are sold in jars. For a few projects you will need acrylic or enamel paints.

HANDY HINTS

Before you varnish a present, make sure you have the right varnish. Use water-based varnish unless otherwise specified.

Put tops back on tightly to keep paints and glue from drying out.

Wash your paintbrushes well after you have used them and store them with the bristles facing upward. Use turpentine to remove oil-based varnish and enamel paints.

Keep modeling materials, such as self-hardening clay or salt dough, in plastic bags to keep them from drying. Keep salt dough in the refrigerator.

You can make presents with more than one material. For example, instead of salt dough you could use self-hardening clay or papier-mâché.

2. There are different brands of self-hardening clay. Read the instructions on the package very carefully to see how long they take to harden in the oven. Some do not need to be baked at all.

3. You can make papier-mâché with wallpaper paste, following the instructions on the package. Or you can just use flour and water (see page 150 for the recipe).

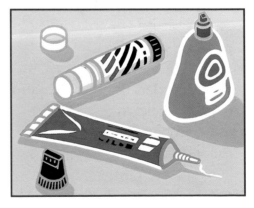

4. To make many of the presents you need glue. Glue sticks are clean and easy to use. Strong glue works best on rubber, cardboard, and paper. Use a fabric glue for fabrics.

NIFTY NAME PLATES

You can make these fancy name plates very easily out of salt, flour, and water. Here are lots of ideas on how to decorate and paint them, and the different shapes and sizes you can make.

Things you need

1½ cups salt, 1½ cups flour, and 1 tbs. oil
½ cup water, baking tray and wax paper
Tempera or poster paints, paintbrushes
Clear varnish and paper clips

Making the dough

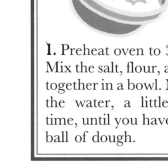

1. Preheat oven to 350°F. Mix the salt, flour, and oil together in a bowl. Mix in the water, a little at a time, until you have a big ball of dough.

2. Put the dough on a floured surface and knead it with your hands until it is very smooth and elastic. If it is too dry, add a little more water.

Nifty name plate

1. Draw the shape of your name plate on wax paper. Sprinkle the paper with flour and then press a lump of dough onto the paper to fill the shape.

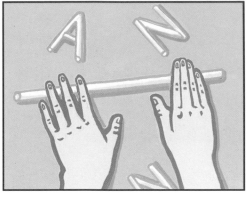

2. To make the letters on your name plate, roll dough into thin sausage shapes. Form each of the sausage shapes into a letter of your name.

3. Carefully press the letters onto your name plate (use a little water to help the dough stick) and add decorations. Push a paper clip into the top, as shown.

4. Put the name plate and wax paper on a baking tray and bake it in the middle of the oven until it is hard. This should take about an hour.

5. Take the name plate out of the oven and wait until it is completely cool. Then paint it with bright tempera or poster paints. Let the paint dry.

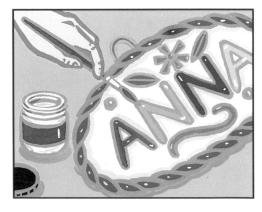

6. Varnish the name plate on the front and let it dry. Then varnish the back. When it is dry, apply another coat of varnish to each side. Let it dry.

HANDY HINTS

Put unused salt dough in a plastic bag and store it in the refrigerator. It will keep for a long time. The more you handle it, the easier it is to use the dough.

Instead of painting the dough after you have baked it, you can stir in food coloring while you make it.

Instead of making a name plate, you can make a picture, such as a kitchen, bedroom, or bathroom scene, to hang on the door.

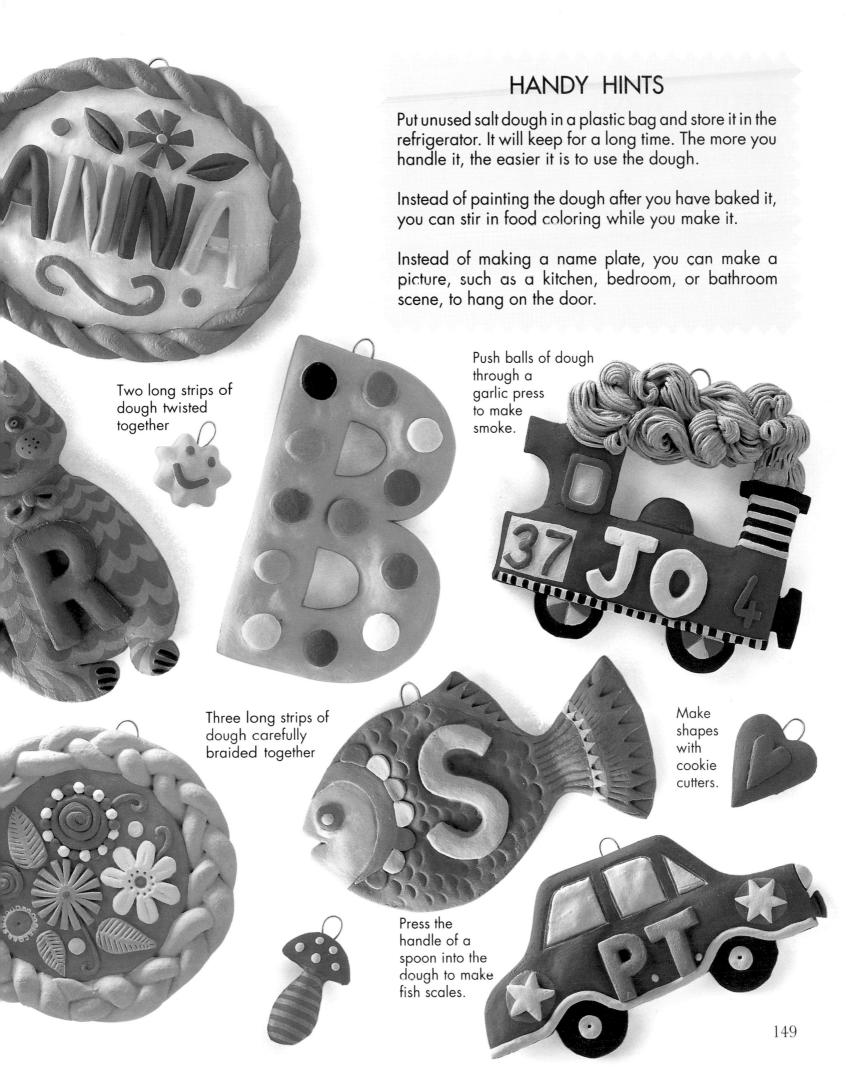

Two long strips of dough twisted together

Push balls of dough through a garlic press to make smoke.

Three long strips of dough carefully braided together

Make shapes with cookie cutters.

Press the handle of a spoon into the dough to make fish scales.

149

PERKY PIGGY BANKS

For a very useful present, you can make a special piggy bank. These are made out of papier-mâché (layers of newspaper and glue) shaped around balloons. You can use different shaped balloons to make various animals, such as a pig, crocodile, or fish. They will take a couple of days to make as each layer of papier-mâché takes a while to dry.

Things you need

Small round balloon
Newspaper
Wallpaper paste
Five corks
Masking tape
Strips of thin cardboard
Scissors
Thin wire (a garbage bag tie is ideal)
Tempera or poster paints
Paintbrush

Perky
pink
pig

Pink pig piggy bank

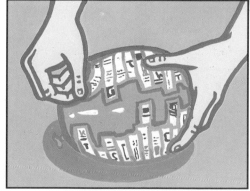

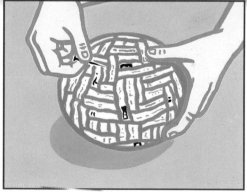

1. Blow up the balloon to the size you want the pig to be. Tie a knot in it. Mix the wallpaper paste, following the instructions on the package. Then tear sheets of newspaper into strips about 1 in. wide and 4 in. long.

2. Cover a strip of paper with paste, wiping off the extra paste between your thumb and first finger. Stick the paper onto the balloon. Do the same with more strips of paper until the balloon is covered. Let dry.

3. Stick six layers of paper onto the balloon, letting each one dry before adding the next. When they are all dry, carefully stick a pin through the papier-mâché shell so that you pop the balloon inside.

150

Fantastic fish money box

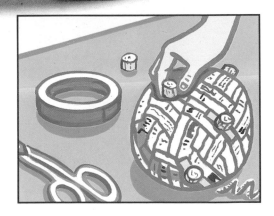

Shape this crazy crocodile around a long, thin balloon. Add a cardboard nose and tail, and cork feet.

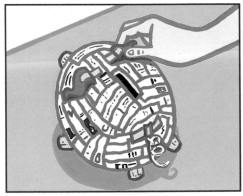

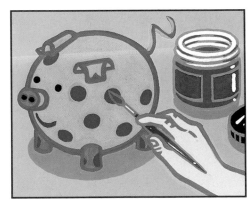

4. Cut one cork in half and tape it onto the papier-mâché shell to make the pig's nose. Tape on the other four corks to make the legs. Shape the wire into a curly tail and cover it with papier-mâché. Tape it onto the body.

5. Cut out two cardboard ears and tape them onto the pig's head. Now stick two more layers of papier-mâché over the pig's body, legs, nose, and ears. Cut a slit in the top to drop the money through.

6. When the pig is completely dry, you can paint it with tempera or poster paints. Brush on a base color first and then let it dry. Decorate the pig and paint on eyes, nostrils, and a mouth.

BRIGHT BUTTONS

Make your own animal, flower, heart, and alphabet buttons out of brightly colored self-hardening clay or painted salt dough. You can sew them onto thick paper and turn them into special birthday and thank-you cards or invitations. Create unusual pictures for presents, too!

Things you need

Self-hardening clay in bright colors
Tracing paper and pencil
Scissors
Thick paper or cardboard
Felt tip pens
Needle and thread
Baking tray and knife
Clear varnish or clear nail polish

Special card for
Valentine's Day

Small number
buttons to sew
on a cardigan

152

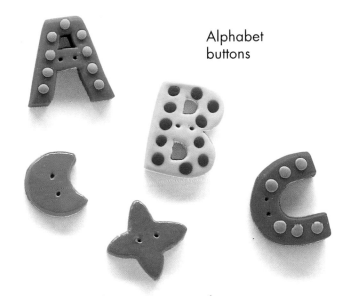

Alphabet buttons

HANDY HINTS

If you do not have any self-hardening clay, make the buttons out of salt dough (see page 148 for the recipe). Paint and varnish the dough buttons when you have baked them.

Instead of making a tracing paper shape to cut around, use tiny cookie cutters in different shapes to make your buttons.

Make a special set of buttons for one of your friends to sew on a cardigan.

Froggy button picture

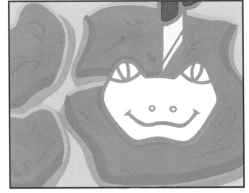

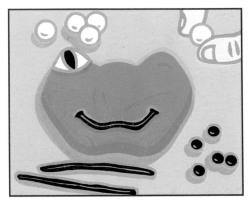

1. Draw a funny frog's face on a sheet of tracing paper, as shown. Cut out the paper frog shape and use it as a pattern.

2. Roll out green self-hardening clay, about as thick as a button. Put the frog shape on the clay and cut around it with a knife. Cut out three frog faces.

3. Roll out six little white balls of clay and six smaller black balls for the frogs' eyes. Press them onto the three faces, as shown. Press on smiley black mouths.

4. Make two holes in the middle with a needle. Put the buttons on a baking tray. Bake them according to the instructions on the package.

5. Take the buttons out of the oven and let them cool. Then paint a layer of varnish on the front of each button. When they are dry, varnish the backs.

6. Fold a piece of cardboard in half. Sew the frog buttons onto the card and draw a picture, such as lily pads, around them with felt tip pens.

PASTA PRESENTS

Brightly painted pasta shapes can be turned into magnificent jewelry very easily. They also make pretty decorations around photograph frames or on a mirror. Try making this pasta bow jewelry box and filling it with pasta jewels.

Things you need

Different pasta shapes — bows,
  spirals, shells, wheels, or animals
Cardboard box
Poster paints (including gold)
Paintbrushes
Clear varnish or nail polish
Thin ribbon or rolled elastic
Scissors and strong glue

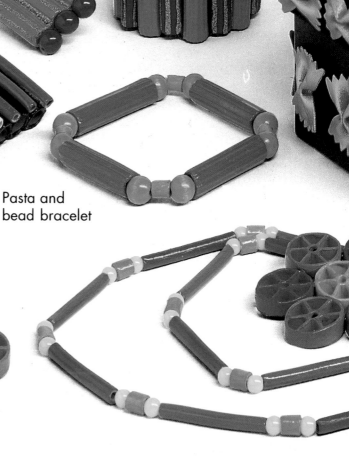

Pasta and
bead bracelet

Perfect pasta
brooches

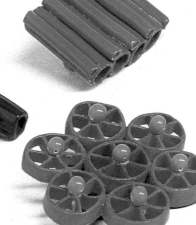

Pasta bow box

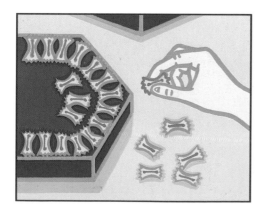

1. Before you start gluing, arrange the pasta bows on the cardboard box to see how they will look and how many you need.

2. Spread glue over the box, a little at a time. Then stick the pasta bows onto the glue. Do this until you have covered the top and sides of the box.

3. When all the bows are stuck firmly onto the box, paint them with gold poster paint. When the paint is dry, paint the bows with clear varnish.

Pasta bow
jewelry box

HANDY HINTS

If you do not have a plain colored box, you can paint it before you start gluing on the pasta.

Always varnish your pasta jewelry after you have painted it. Otherwise it might get soggy if it gets wet or damp.

To make pasta jewelry look very rich, paint it with gold or silver paint, cover it with glue, and dip it in glitter. You can also use glitter glue.

Pretty
pasta tube
necklace

Pretty pasta necklace

1. Paint some long and short spiral pasta tubes with bright poster paints. It is best to paint the tubes half at a time and then let them dry.

2. When the paint is absolutely dry, carefully brush a thick layer of clear nail polish over each one of the pasta tubes. Let the polish dry completely.

3. Cut a piece of thin ribbon a little longer than you want the necklace to be. Thread the painted pasta onto the ribbon and tie the ends in a bow.

PAINTED PLATES

Painted plates make wonderful presents to hang on the wall! You can paint them with bright patterns or pictures, for Christmas, birthdays, or a new baby. It is best to use glazed china plates and special enamel or acrylic paints. You can find them in most craft and art supply stores.

Things you need

Paper, a pencil, and colored pens
White glazed china plate
China marker
Paintbrushes and turpentine
Enamel or acrylic paints in
  bright colors
Saucers to mix paints

Hang your funny feast plate in the kitchen.

Clown plate for a baby

Paint a pattern instead of a picture.

156

Funny feast

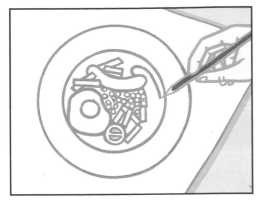

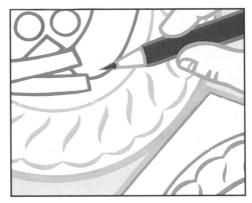

1. For practice, trace your plate on paper. Draw and color a fried egg, two sausages, a tomato, french fries, and peas, as shown.

2. Turn the picture around to make sure it looks good from all angles. Copy the design onto a plain glazed plate, using a china marker.

3. If you are using enamel paints, stir them well before you begin to paint. Do not mix colors. Start by painting in a background color, as shown.

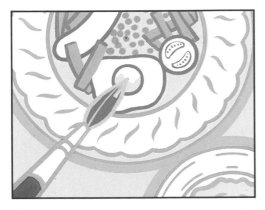

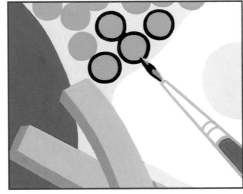

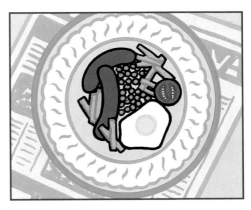

4. When the background color is completely dry, paint in the rest of your design. Do not put too much paint on the brush, but gradually build up the color.

5. When you have finished painting, put the plate on newspaper to dry completely. Using a thin brush, add a black outline to the picture.

6. You will have to be very careful and keep a steady hand when you outline your picture. You can outline it in any color or not at all if you prefer.

HANDY HINTS

Read the instructions carefully before you use your paints as different brands of enamel paint dry in different ways.

Never eat off your painted plates or put them in the dishwasher as the hot water may make them peel. Wash them with dish-washing liquid.

Make sure you have lots of turpentine for washing your brushes and thinning your paint. You can wipe off your mistakes with a soft cloth dipped in turpentine.

Try using acrylic paints. They are not as shiny as enamels, but they dry more quickly.

FABULOUS FRAMES

Everybody loves being given photographs of their family, friends, or pets, especially if they are nicely framed. Try making these fabulous frames out of cardboard decorated with metal or tinfoil. You can also make shiny foil Christmas decorations and candleholders.

Things you need

Paper, pencil, and ruler
Cardboard, scissors, and masking tape
Metal foil from an empty tomato
   paste tube, or tinfoil cut from a
   clean foil baking tray
Photograph
Ballpoint pen
Strong glue or glue stick

Tomato paste
tube frame

Shiny Christmas
tree decorations

Tinfoil frame

158

Design your own candleholders.

HANDY HINTS

Instead of using metal foil from a tomato paste tube, you can cut up a tinfoil baking tray to decorate your frames. You can make a big frame out of a big, shallow baking tray.

Before you start decorating the foil, decide what pattern you are going to design. Remember to press hard with a ballpoint pen.

Heart frame

1. Cut the lid off an empty tomato paste tube with scissors. Cut the tube open and wash it out. Flatten it with your hand — be careful of sharp edges. Let the foil dry.

2. Draw a heart shape, about 5 in. high, on cardboard. It should be no bigger than your piece of foil. Draw a rectangle, about 4 in. long and 1 in. wide. Cut out both cardboard shapes.

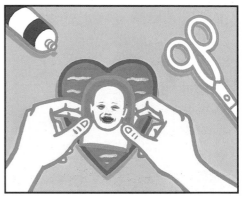

3. Cut out the photograph you want to frame and glue it to the middle of the cardboard heart, as shown. It is probably best to cut out just the face so it will show through the frame.

4. Using the tips of your scissors, score a line across the rectangular cardboard shape, about 1 in. from one end. Fold it over and tape it to the back of the heart shape with masking tape.

5. Trace the cardboard heart shape onto the written side of the metal foil with a ballpoint pen. Cut it out. Draw a smaller heart in the middle of the foil, as shown, and cut it out.

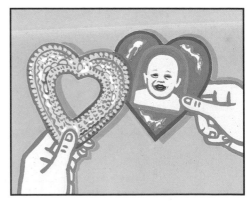

6. Using a ballpoint pen, draw patterns on the back of the foil heart. Press hard. Stick the heart, shiny side up, onto the cardboard heart, with the photograph showing through.

MERRY MOBILES

Colorful mobiles make great presents
for babies because they love to look
at interesting things that move about.
Try choosing a theme, such as
animals, monsters, or these birds,
when you are designing your mobile.
Use bright colors and simple shapes.

Make the
birds as
colorful as
possible.

Things you need

Paper and pencil
10 squares of felt in
  bright colors
Needle and strong thread
Fabric glue
Scissors and pins
Lampshade ring or
  wooden embroidery ring
Colored thread
  or yarn

Bright bird mobile

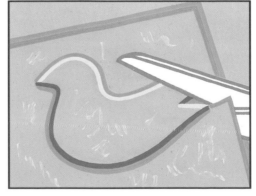

1. Draw a simple bird shape, as
shown, on thin cardboard. Cut it
out. Put the shape on a felt
square and draw around it. Cut
out a felt bird.

2. Glue the felt bird onto a felt
square and cut around it so you
have a double-thick felt bird.
Make ten birds out of different-
colored felt.

3. Now draw a wing shape, as
shown, on thin cardboard. Cut it
out. Put it on felt and cut around
it. Cut out ten pairs of wings in
different colors.

HANDY HINTS

You can make the felt animals with or without stuffing in the middle. The stuffing makes them a little bit thicker and stiffer.

Instead of gluing the felt shapes together, try sewing them together with bright thread.

Look in picture books to get ideas for your mobile and for simple shapes to copy.

Magic moons
and stars mobile

Monster
mobile

4. Glue a wing onto each side of every felt bird. Then cut 20 eyes and 20 beaks out of the felt. Glue them onto both sides of each bird. Let the glue dry.

5. Sew a long piece of colored thread with a knot in one end to the middle of each bird, as shown. Tie the birds at different lengths around the lampshade ring.

6. Tie three pieces of thread, about 1 ft. long, around the ring. Knot the ends together. Hang up the mobile and move the birds until it balances.

BRILLIANT BEADS

On these two pages you can find out how to make all sorts of beads from self-hardening clay. Most craft and art supply stores sell it in bright colors. You can mix colors together to make exciting and interesting patterns. Try making your own designs and shapes.

Things you need

Self-hardening clay in bright colors
Toothpick
Thin colored string or ribbon

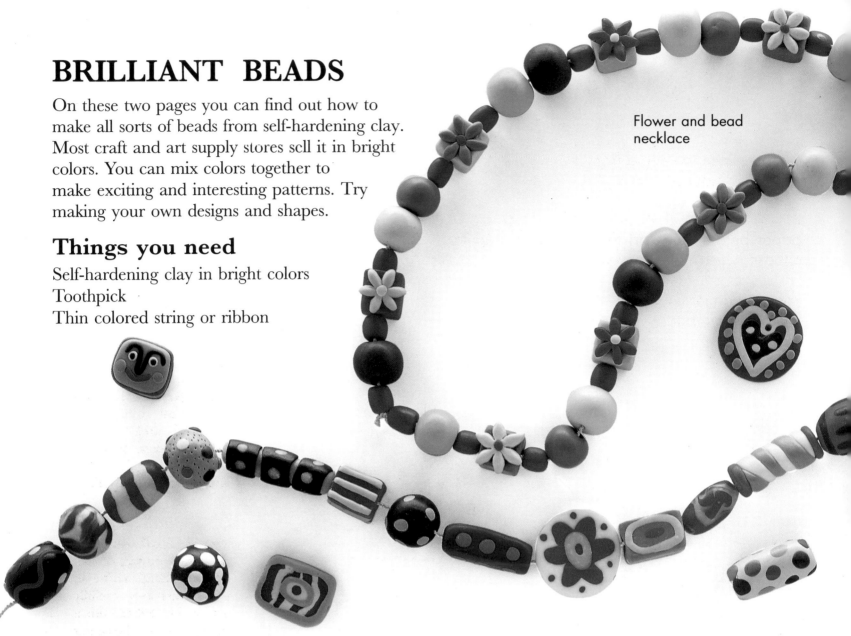

Flower and bead necklace

Big bright necklace

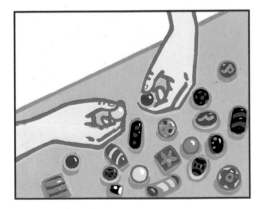

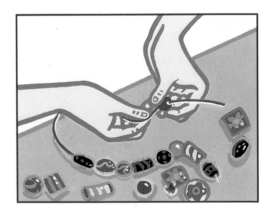

1. Choose the big bright beads you want to make, or design beads of your own. Try making them in lots of different shapes, sizes, colors and patterns.

2. Push a toothpick through each bead so you can thread it. Put the beads on a baking tray. Bake according to the instructions on the package.

3. When the beads are cool, decide which ones you want to put next to each other to make a necklace or bracelet. Thread the beads on colored string.

162

HANDY HINTS

It's easier to mold self-hardening clay once you have softened it in your hands. Roll it out on a clean surface to keep it from getting dirty, and keep the colors separate.

It helps to draw the design of your beads on paper before you start to make them, and to choose which colors you want to use.

You can varnish your beads once they are baked to make them brighter and shiny.

Roll out long, thin strips of clay to decorate different shapes, like these fish and wheels.

Big bright beads

To make this bead, roll out very thin strips of clay and make tiny balls. Press them on to a square bead to make a face.

To make a flower, flatten a small ball of clay. Cut out six wedges with a knife. Then mold the petals with your fingers.

To make a striped bead, make two separate beads in different colors. Slice the beads and then put them together, first one color and then the other. Roll until it is smooth.

To make this flower, press five little triangles of clay onto a flat bead in a flower shape. Then very carefully flatten the flower with a rolling pin. Add the center and the stripes.

To make a marbled bead, mix two colors together in a ball. Roll the ball until it is completely smooth.

To make a bead with swirls flatten two small balls of different colors. Roll them together like a jelly roll. Cut off thin slices, press them on a big bead, and roll until smoothed.

FUNNY FAMILY FIGURINES

For an original present, try making funny figurines of your family and friends — even your pets! You can make them out of salt dough (see page 148 for the recipe). The figurines look even funnier if you give each person a special feature that reminds you especially of them.

Things you need

Salt dough (see page 148)
Tempera or poster paints
Paintbrushes
Clear varnish or nail polish
Garlic press
Toothpick
Pencil
Baking tray

Make an angel Christmas decoration.

Make a nice fat Santa Claus.

Figurine of Mom

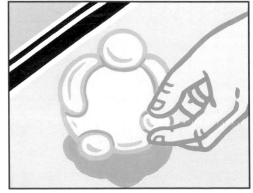

1. Draw a picture of the person you want to make, or use a photograph. The figurine must have a solid body, as shown, to stand on when it is baked.

2. Roll a big ball of dough for the body and press it onto a baking tray. Press on a smaller ball for the head. Make sausage-shaped arms and round feet.

3. When you have made the body, add the features. Push balls of dough through a garlic press for the hair. Press on a nose and mouth.

Family of salt dough figurines

HANDY HINTS

Salt dough figurines take different lengths of time to harden in the oven depending on how big and fat they are. It is best to check them while they are cooking. Small figures take about 30 to 40 minutes.

Knead the dough well before you use it. The softer it is, the easier it is to use.

It's best to make your models short and fat rather than tall, as they spread out when they are baking.

4. Use a toothpick to poke holes for the eyes and to make finger lines. Add something special that reminds you of the person, such as a particular dress or tie.

5. Let the figurine dry out a little. Then put it in the oven at 350°F until it is hard. Take it out and let it cool. Paint it with bright poster or tempera paints.

6. When the paint is dry, varnish the figurine all over and let dry. Then brush another coat of varnish onto the front and back. Let dry.

165

MARVELOUS MAGNETS

These nifty magnets are easy and fun to make and are super presents for people of all ages. They stick on any metal surface, such as a refrigerator or a filing cabinet, and are useful for holding up notes, lists, and pictures.

Things you need

Candies, such as brightly colored jelly beans or lollipops

Small, round magnets (available from hardware stores)

Mini baking cups and strong glue

Clear varnish and paintbrush

Small bright objects make the best and prettiest magnets. You will probably be able to find lots of good objects to use around the house. Most things just need a magnet stuck on the back, but some may need to be varnished.

HANDY HINTS

Allow lots of time for the coats of varnish to dry on your magnets. Start making them a few days before you want to give them away as presents.

If you are using cookies or candies, it is best to let them dry out before you varnish them.

Before you start, varnish a candy to test the color.

Pretty present magnets

Bright bow magnet

Magnets made from modeling clay

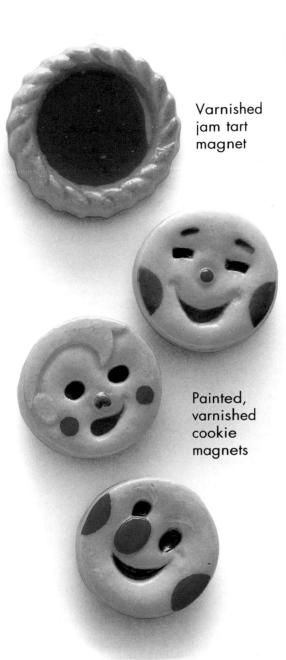

Varnished jam tart magnet

Painted, varnished cookie magnets

A basketful of flowers

Use many different kinds of candy.

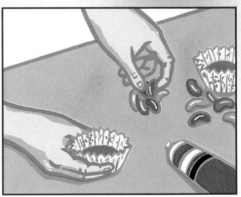

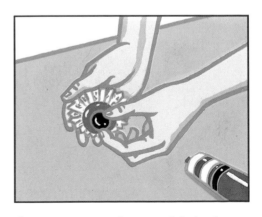

Jelly bean magnet

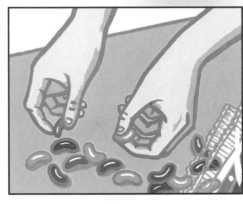

1. Arrange some jelly beans in a baking cup to see how many you need. Make sure they are not too heavy for the size of magnet you are going to use.

2. Glue the jelly beans together with strong glue and let them dry. Stick them into two mini baking cups, one inside the other. Let the glue dry.

3. Cover completely with clear varnish. Let dry and then varnish again three or four times. Make sure the varnish dries between each coat.

4. As soon as the varnish is dry and hard, stick a magnet onto the bottom of the mini baking cup. Let it dry. Now try making other kinds of magnets.

167

FELT PICTURES

These fantastic felt pictures make perfect presents for moms, dads, and grandparents. They are made out of pieces of colored felt stuck or sewn on top of each other. They can also be decorated with buttons, beads, and bright embroidery thread. If you don't have any felt, you can use another kind of fabric instead.

Things you need

Drawing paper
Tracing paper
Pencil and eraser
Scissors
Fabric glue
Squares of felt in different colors
Sewing pins

My dad

Cool cat picture

1. On a sheet of paper, draw the picture you are going to make in the same size as you want it to be. Start with something simple, such as this cool cat.

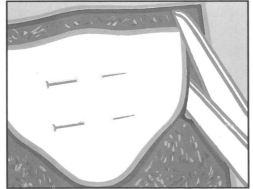

2. Trace the cat's face onto tracing paper and cut it out. Use this as a paper pattern. Pin the paper pattern onto a square of felt and cut around it.

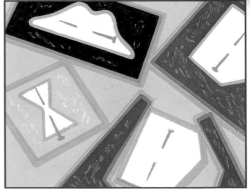

3. Now trace the cat's hat, bow tie, shirt, and coat. Cut them out separately. Pin each paper pattern onto a different felt square and cut them out.

168

Cool cat

My house

4. Using fabric glue, stick the felt cat's face onto a big square of felt of a different color. Then glue on the hat, bow tie, shirt, and coat, as shown. Let the glue dry.

5. Cut out and glue some long whiskers on the cat's cheeks. Trace and cut out sunglasses and glue them on the cat's face. Glue a band on the hat.

6. Cut out small pieces of felt for the nose, mouth, and ears and glue them on. Add different-colored lapels and a pocket handkerchief to the coat.

BEAUTIFUL BOWS

These beautiful bows are very easy to make with just newspaper, glue, and paint. They can be made into brooches and earrings, or turned into colorful cuff links. Decorated with poster paints and then varnished, they can be stuck onto hair bands, hair combs, or shoes.

Things you need

Newspaper
Wallpaper paste
Bowl of water
Tempera or poster paints and
    paintbrush
Clear gloss varnish
    or nail polish
Strong glue (for sticking
    on brooch backs,
    earrings, cuff links, or
    hair combs)
Brooch back

Paper bow
brooch

Polka-dot
paper
bow tie

Beautiful bow
hair combs

Pretty
paper bow
brooch

170

Snappy shoe bows

HANDY HINTS

If you stick several layers of paper together at the same time, they will take longer to dry, but the papier-mâché will be much stronger.

Remember to decide what size to make the bow before you start. Big bows are best for bow ties and brooches, medium-size ones look good on hair bands or hair combs. Smaller bows make pretty earrings, cuff links and shoe bows.

Paper bow brooch

1. Mix the wallpaper paste following the instructions on the package. Then rip large sheets of newspaper into quarters and soak them, one by one, in cold water, for a few seconds.

2. Take the paper out of the water and lay it flat on a table. Peel off the top strip and spread paste over it with your hands or a paintbrush. Carefully rip the glued paper in half lengthways.

3. Stick one half of the paper to the other so that an unglued side sticks to a glued one. Do this again so you have a long strip of paper four layers deep. Cut off a strip at one end.

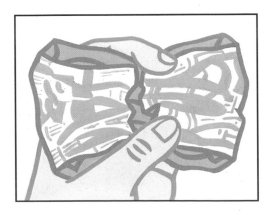

4. Fold in the edges of the long strip to neaten them. Then fold the two ends into the middle to make a bow shape, as shown. Pinch the middle to make the bow look nice and full.

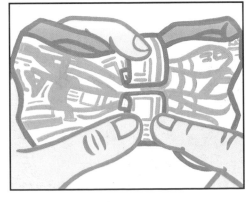

5. Now fold in the edges of the little strip to neaten them. Wrap the strip around the bow so that it covers the join in the middle. Fold the ends under and leave the bow to dry.

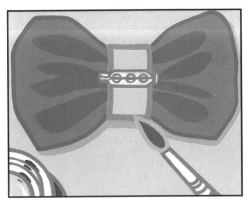

6. When it is dry, decorate the bow with poster paint. Let it dry and then paint on a pattern. Stick the bow onto a brooch back with strong glue. Then varnish it to make it look shiny.

PICTURE PRESENTS

Old boxes and tin cans can be made to look beautiful by decorating them with lots of tiny pictures or patterns cut out from postcards, glossy magazines, birthday cards, or wrapping paper, and then varnished. You can also try decorating hairbrushes, hand mirrors, and photograph frames with cut-out pictures.

Things you need

Box or tin can
Old magazines, wrapping paper,
  birthday cards, or postcards
Small scissors
Strong glue or glue stick
Clear varnish
Fine sandpaper
Paintbrush
Soft cloth

Make a frame to cover with pictures.

Picture box

Cover a box for Dad with old stamps and varnish.

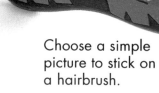

Choose a simple picture to stick on a hairbrush.

172

Pretty picture box

1. Before you start, make sure that the box or tin can is clean and smooth so that it is ready to decorate. Peel off any labels or bumpy bits.

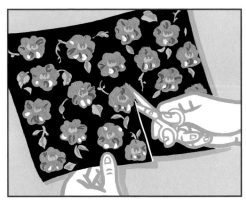

2. Using a pair of small, sharp scissors, carefully cut out the pictures you want to cover the box with. To start with, practice cutting out bigger pictures.

3. Arrange the pictures on the box and then glue on the first one. Rub hard to get rid of any air bubbles and to make a smooth surface.

4. Wipe off extra glue with a soft cloth and glue on the next picture. Continue until you have covered the box with little pictures. Let the glue dry.

5. Once the glue has dried you can begin to varnish. Brush on the first coat and let it dry overnight. Then gently sand it down with fine sandpaper.

6. Dust the box and then varnish on another coat. Let each coat dry before adding the next. You will need ten layers of varnish. Do not sand the last coat.

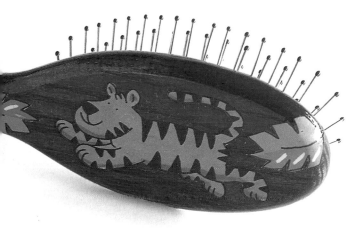

HANDY HINTS

It's best to use good quality pictures to decorate presents. Save wrapping paper, postcards, and Christmas and birthday cards.

Before you start, decide what kinds of pictures you are going to use, such as birds or flowers. You can also use old stamps and even shells, buttons, sequins, or beads.

GLORIOUS GLOVES

Here's a really different kind of present to give to someone to make them laugh. You can buy cheap dish-washing gloves and cotton gloves in many bright colors from hardware or grocery stores to make these crazy gloves.

Things you need

for dish-washing gloves

Two pairs of rubber gloves
 in different colors
Plastic shopping bag
Needle, thread, and pins
Strong glue
Scissors and pencil

for dust glove

Cotton glove
Dust rag or cloth
Felt for the nails
Diamantés and sequins
Fabric glue or needle
 and thread

Cut circles out of balloons to decorate the gloves.

Wild dish-washing gloves

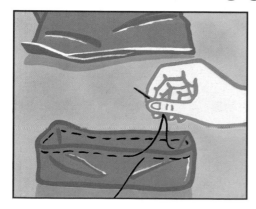

1. Cut a strip, about 3 in. wide and 15 in. long, out of a plastic bag. Thread a needle and sew a running stitch as close to one edge as possible, as shown.

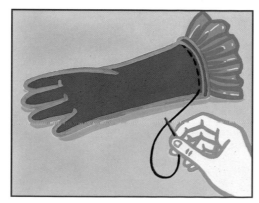

2. Take out the needle and pull up the thread to make a frilly cuff. When it is small enough to fit around a rubber glove, pin it and sew it on, as shown.

3. Repeat with the other glove of the same color. Then cut out ten fingernails and flowers from the different-colored glove. Stick them on the gloves with glue.

174

Dainty dust glove

Grisly gardening gloves

HANDY HINTS

Before you start decorating your dish-washing gloves, test the glue to make sure it sticks.

Be careful not to stick or sew the front of the glove to the back when you are putting the dust rag on the dusting glove.

Try sticking diamanté shapes onto the dish-washing gloves to make them look fancy.

Dainty dust glove

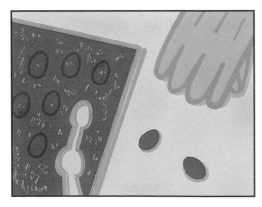

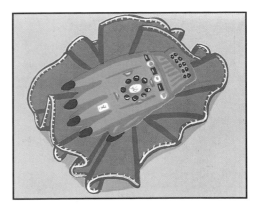

1. Draw five fingernails on the felt. Make sure they are big enough to fit on the ends of the fingers of the cotton glove. Cut them out.

2. Using fabric glue, stick one felt nail onto the tip of each finger of the cotton glove, as shown. Let the glue dry.

3. Carefully stick or sew the dust rag to the middle of the glove, as shown. Then stick or sew bright diamantés and sequins onto the glove to decorate it.

SWEET PRESENTS

When you do not have much time to make a present, why not give some delicious homemade candies? These are very quick to make, as you don't have to cook them. You can make them even more special by putting them in a pretty box or basket tied with a bow.

Things you need
for the marzipan fruits*

1 cup almond paste
1 whipped egg white
1½ cups powdered sugar
Lemon juice
Food coloring
Bowl, wooden spoon
  and fork

for coconut ice

2½ cups powdered sugar
1 teaspoon of vanilla extract
Small can of condensed milk
¼ cup shredded coconut
Red food coloring
2 bowls
Wooden spoon
Baking pan and knife

Fill a tiny basket with all kinds of marzipan fruits.

Put the coconut ice in mini baking cups in a box.

*Ready-made marzipan may be used if salmonella poisoning is a concern.

176

Marzipan fruits

1. Gradually add almond paste to whipped egg white. Add powdered sugar. If the mixture is too dry, add lemon juice, a little at a time, until you have a soft ball of marzipan.

2. Divide the marzipan into four separate lumps. Put each lump into a bowl. Then add a few drops of a different color food coloring to each bowl. Mix it well with a fork.

3. Shape the marzipan mixture into fruits — red for strawberries and plums, yellow for bananas and lemons, green for apples and pears. Use cloves for stalks and green marzipan to make leaves.

Make lines on the bananas.

Dip the strawberries in sugar.

Roll the oranges around the outside of a fine grater.

Coconut ice

1. Sift the sugar into a bowl and then add the vanilla extract and condensed milk. Add the shredded coconut and stir the mixture with a wooden spoon until it becomes stiff.

2. Divide the mixture in half and put one half in the second bowl. Add a few drops of red food coloring to one of the mixtures and stir it until it becomes pale pink.

3. Put the white mixture in the bottom of the baking pan. Put it in the refrigerator until firm. Spread the pink mixture on top and put it in the refrigerator. When it is hard, cut into squares.

GREAT GINGERBREAD PRESENTS

Gingerbread is simple to make and delicious to eat. You can make it into almost any shape you like, such as gingerbread people and animals, a gingerbread house, decorations to hang on a Christmas tree, and even name plates for your friends and family.

Things you need

1¼ cups self-rising flour
1 tablespoon ground ginger
6 tablespoons butter
¼ cup corn syrup
½ cup soft brown sugar
3 tablespoons milk
Margarine or oil (for greasing baking tray)
Flour (for flouring work top)
Tube of ready-made icing
Sifter, large bowl, and a wooden spoon
Rolling pin and baking tray
Cookie cutters in different shapes and sizes
Toothpick

Gingerbread family

Making the gingerbread

1. Preheat oven to 325°F. Sift the flour and ginger together into the bowl. Then, using your fingertips, rub the butter into the mixture.

2. Mix the syrup, sugar, and milk together and add them to the flour mixture. Mix them into a dough. Put the dough in the refrigerator for an hour.

3. Grease the baking tray with oil or margarine. Lightly flour the work space and roll out the dough with a rolling pin to a thickness of about ¼ in.

178

Gingerbread Christmas decorations

Gingerbread name plates

Gingerbread animals

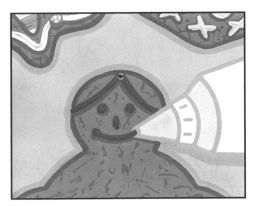

4. Using cookie cutters, cut out some gingerbread cookies. Put them on the baking tray, leaving gaps between the shapes to allow them to spread.

5. Make a small hole near the top of each shape with a toothpick. Bake cookies in the oven for 10 to 15 minutes, or until they are golden brown.

6. When the gingerbread cookies are cool, draw faces, names, or patterns on them with the icing. Thread ribbon through the holes before you give them away.

PAPER BOWLS

These colorful bowls are made out of papier-mâché. They make wonderful fruit bowls, pencil and pen holders, or special vases for flowers. You can paint your own designs on them or decorate them with colored sugar or tissue paper.

Papier-mâché a jam jar to make a waterproof vase. Keep the jar in place for the water.

Things you need

Large bowl (to use as a mold)
Plastic wrap or petroleum jelly
Newspaper
Wallpaper paste
Bowl for mixing glue
Paintbrush and water
Tempera or poster paints
Scissors
Clear varnish

Perfect paper bowl

Perfect paper bowl

1. Cover the outside of the bowl you are using as a mold with plastic wrap. Make sure that the plastic wrap covers the edge of the bowl. This will stop the papier-mâché from sticking to the edge.

2. Mix the wallpaper paste, following the instructions on the package.

3. Tear the newspaper into big pieces. Drop them, one by one, into 3 in. of water in a sink. Wet them for five minutes and then carefully take them out. Lay them down on a work surface.

180

HANDY HINTS

Instead of using plastic wrap, you can use petroleum jelly to stop the papier-mâché from sticking to the bowl.

If the papier-mâché shell tears when you take it off the bowl, fix it with masking tape. Papier-mâché over the tear.

To make a pencil holder, papier-mâché an old salt canister or box. Separate it from the plastic wrap with a dinner knife.

4. Tear the wet newspaper into small strips. Cover the outside of the bowl with a layer of strips. Make sure that they overlap so that they cover the plastic wrap. Brush the paste over the strips.

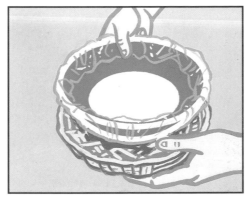

5. Cover the paste with more strips. Let it dry. Add more paste and paper until you have five or six layers of papier-mâché. When it is dry, separate the paper and paste shell from the bowl.

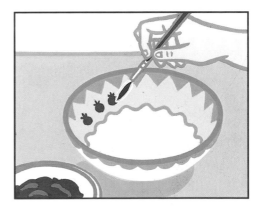

6. Trim the edges with scissors. Paint the bowl all over with tempera or poster paints. When it is dry, paint on bright patterns. To give it a glossy look, brush on a layer of clear varnish.

COLORFUL CANDLEHOLDERS

For special occasions, such as Christmas, birthday parties, or even spooky Halloween parties, it is fun to have candles burning on the table. Try making these colorful salt dough candleholders to help decorate the table.

Things you need

Ready-made salt dough (see page 148)
Rolling pin, knife, and baking tray
Round cookie cutters or a glass
Thin cardboard and scissors
Tempera or poster paints and
  paintbrush
Clear varnish or nail polish
Strong glue and Plasticine
Two thin candles

Slithery snake candleholder

Deep candleholder filled with candies

Holders for thick candles

Christmas candleholder

Spooky Halloween holder

Christmas candleholders

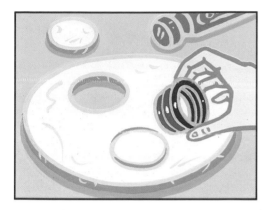

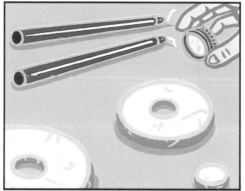

1. Turn the oven on to 350°F. Roll out the dough until it is about ½ in. thick. Cut out two circles of dough with a round cookie cutter or a glass.

2. Cut out a circle in the middle of the round shapes of dough a little bigger than the end of a candle. Use a small round cookie cutter or a bottle top.

3. Cut out salt dough holly leaves and roll small balls to make the berries. Stick them around the circle of dough with water, as shown.

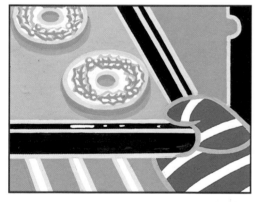

4. Put the Christmas rings in the oven on a baking tray until they are hard. This should take about an hour. Take them out and let them cool completely.

5. When they are cool, put the rings on a piece of cardboard and draw around them. Cut out the circles. Glue them to the bottom of the rings, as shown.

6. Paint the candleholders with poster paints. When the paint is dry, brush on a layer of varnish. Stick Plasticine in the holes and press in the candles.

HANDY HINTS

Let the salt dough candleholders dry out a little before you bake them in the oven.

Instead of using cookie cutters, you can cut out the dough rings with jar lids or ramekin dishes.

You can make little bowls for your candles by covering an upturned ramekin dish with salt dough and baking it in the oven. Be very careful not to break the salt dough shell when you take it off the ramekin dish.

POTTED PLANT STICKS

For an unusual present, especially for people who love flowers and gardening, you can make these potted plant sticks. They are very useful for propping up flowers in a potted plant and they help drain the water through the soil.

Things you need

Thin wooden sticks about 8 in. long
  (thin dowels or garden markers
  are best)
Scraps of colored felt
Self-hardening clay in bright colors
Fabric glue and baking tray
Pencil and paper

Spooky
glow-in-the-dark
skull stick

Felt flower
plant sticks

Two-faced
pig stick

Modeling
clay fish
stick

Use glow-in-the-
dark modeling
clay to make this
spooky spider.

184

HANDY HINTS

Use old lollipop sticks to make plant sticks for tiny pots. They also make good table decorations for parties.

Try making some spooky plant sticks with special glow-in-the-dark clay or paint.

Salt dough (see page 148), papier-mâché animals, flowers, bows, and thick painted cardboard shapes make good potted plant sticks.

Felt flower plant stick

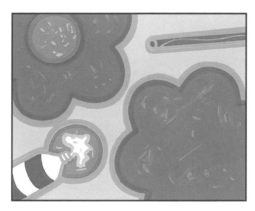

1. Draw a flower on paper and cut it out. Pin the shape on felt and cut around it. Do this again. Cut out two felt leaves and two flower centers.

2. Spread glue on one side of each flower center and stick them onto the middle of the flower shapes, as shown. Leave the glue to dry completely.

3. Glue the flowers together, as shown, with the top of the stick sandwiched between them. Glue the leaves together with the stick between one end.

Two-faced pig stick

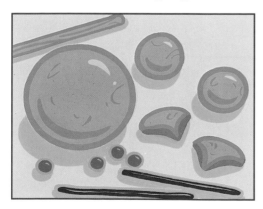

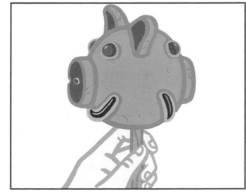

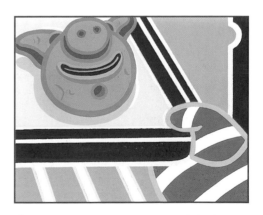

1. Roll a ball of bright pink self-hardening clay for the pig's head and two smaller balls for its noses. Make four little blue eyes, two pink ears, and two black mouths.

2. Press a nose, two eyes, and a mouth onto each side of the head. Put on the ears. Push a stick into the head where the neck would be, about 1 in. deep.

3. Take the stick out and bake the pig's head in the oven according to the instructions on the package. Before the clay cools, push the stick back into the hole.

CRAZY STRING HOLDERS

Turn your empty yogurt containers or plastic tubs into these crazy animal heads. Fixed to the wall, they make great holders for string, ribbon, and yarn. You can use all sorts of different shaped and sized pots, which you can probably find around the house.

Things you need

Empty plastic containers
Thin cardboard (an old cereal
  box is ideal)
Acrylic paints and paintbrush
Pencil
Scissors and thumbtacks
Small balls of string, ribbon,
  or yarn
Strong glue or glue stick
Beads

Striped tiger
string holder

Striped tiger holder

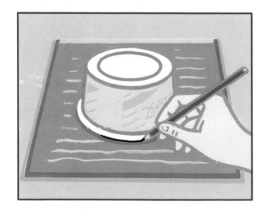

1. Wash out an empty yogurt container. Soak it in water and peel off any labels. When it is dry, trace the container onto some thin cardboard, as shown.

2. For the striped tiger, add big round ears. Carefully cut around them and the cardboard shape. Then cut a flap, as shown, in the middle of the cardboard shape.

3. Cover the container with a thick layer of white acrylic paint. Let it dry. Then paint on a layer of orange paint and let it dry. Paint on the stripes, as shown.

Big bull holder

HANDY HINTS

Do not put a big ball of string or yarn into your crazy string holder as it may be too heavy and will pull the holder off the wall.

You can put all sorts of things onto your string heads to make them look even crazier. Use cotton balls for sheep, yarn for a horse's mane, buttons for noses, and beads for eyes.

Happy pig holder

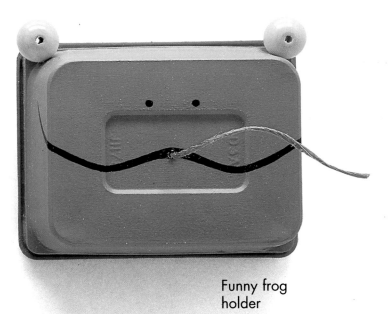

Funny frog holder

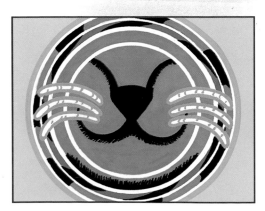

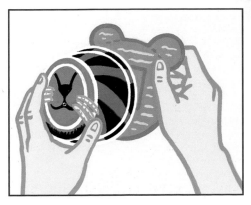

4. When the paint is dry, paint on the tiger's nose and mouth. Make sure the mouth is where you want the string to come out. Glue on some string whiskers.

5. Using small scissors, poke a hole in the mouth. Then glue the cardboard shape onto the back of the container. Paint the tiger's ears orange and black.

6. Glue on bead eyes. Put some string into the container. Pull one end through the mouth. To stick the holder on the wall, push a thumbtack through each ear.

WRAPPING IT UP

Now that you have made your presents, it's very important to know how to wrap them up properly to make them look super special. Here are some wonderful wrapping ideas and ways to decorate your presents with bows and paper ribbons. Instead of buying paper you could try to make your own.

Things you need

Wrapping paper
Clear tape
Scissors
Thin paper ribbon
Sheets of paper in
    different colors

Use a potato or stencil to print patterns on homemade wrapping paper.

You can make long, tricky-shaped presents look like real crackers. Tie bows around the ends.

Perfect present

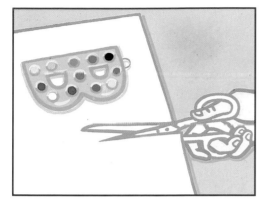

1. Put the present on a sheet of wrapping paper to see how much you need. Make sure you have enough to fold in both ends and to overlap the paper at the top. Cut the paper.

2. Put the present facedown on the paper. Fold the long edges over the top so that they overlap. Make sure the paper is tight before you tape it.

3. Turn one end of the present toward you and fold in the ends as neatly as possible to make corner folds, as shown. Tape them down. Do the same to the other end of the paper.

Curls and bows

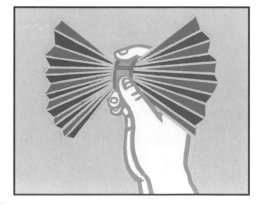

1. Decorate your present with curly paper ribbon. To make the ribbon curl, hold it between your thumb and the blade of a pair of scissors. Firmly pull the blade along the ribbon.

2. You can make your own paper curls by cutting out strips of paper and wrapping them around a wooden spoon or stick. Try using different widths and colors.

3. Make a pleated paper bow by folding some paper over and over again like an accordion. Pinch the middle and wrap a strip of paper around it. Tape or glue it.

Make gift tags out of colored paper. Tie them on with thin ribbon.

HANDY HINTS

To make your packages look best, fold in the sides and ends of your paper before you start to wrap.

If you don't have any wrapping paper you can use newspaper comics or tinfoil. Decorating plain paper with potato prints or stencils is also nice.